Anglican Religious Communities Year Book

1999

Published by **Canterbury Press Norwich**
a publishing imprint of Hymns Ancient & Modern Limited
(a registered charity)
St Mary's Works, St Mary's Plain, Norwich, Norfolk, NR3 3BH

The cover design is by Leigh Hurlock.

Line drawings are by Sister Anna Huston SSM .

A catalogue record for this book is available
from the British Library.

North American Edition, 1998
Forward Movement Publications,
412 Sycamore Street,
Cincinati. Ohio 45202–4195 USA

ISBN 0–88028–199–5
Order No: 1479

```
       COKESBURY  VTS  33600
   01/30/99  13:42   F     18    5411

   Customer Account Record # 0012631016
   Charge to Account # 5641538

   GLEASON RICHARD J
   6510 KOZIARA DR

   BURKE, VA 22015
   Telephone # (703) 644-2458

   ORDERED BY SAME

      1 @   7.95 0880281995 30%$    5.57
                ANGLICAN RELIGIOUS COMMU
   SUBTOTAL                    $    5.57
   TAX      @ 4.5000%          $    0.25
   TOTAL                       $    5.82
   TENDERED Cash   0012631016  $   20.00
   CHANGE                      $   14.18

     EVENING HOURS ON TUES & THURS 10-8 PM
   M,W,F   10-5:30 SAT 10-5  1-800-368-3756
```

```
      COKESBURY  VTS  33600
  01/30/99   13:42   F     18      5411

  Customer Account Record # 0012631016
  Charge to Account # 5641538

  GLEASON RICHARD J
  6510 KOZIARA DR

  BURKE, VA 22015
  Telephone # (703) 644-2458

  ORDERED BY SAME

    1 @   7.95 0880281995 30%$    5.57
               ANGLICAN RELIGIOUS COMMU
  SUBTOTAL                    $    5.57
  TAX      @ 4.5000%          $    0.25
  TOTAL                       $    5.82
  TENDERED Cash   0012631016  $   20.00
  CHANGE                      $   14.18

   EVENING HOURS ON TUES & THURS 10-8 PM
  M,W,F   10-5:30 SAT 10-5  1-800-368-3756
```

Contents

Foreword

by
The Archbishop of Canterbury

Some years ago, I referred to the Religious Communities within the Church of England as 'one of our best kept secrets'. I became aware just how well kept this secret is when I paid an official visit to Georgia and sat next to the distinguished Patriarch of that significant Church. I happened to mention that two Anglican nuns were important members of my staff. The Patriarch was visibly stirred. Thereafter, his whole approach to the Church of England was transformed by his discovery of the presence of monastic life in our Church.

Celebrating this 'secret' of Anglican communities, so that their life and work becomes better known, is important for the whole Church. I welcome this new Year Book, therefore, as both a directory of information and also, through its news items and articles, as a window on the many and diverse ministries in which communities engage. Some are involved in social projects, others in a ministry of hospitality, and some live a hidden life of contemplation. All are centred in a life of prayer, which is a deep encouragement to the Church.

I commend this Year Book and hope it gains a wide readership. The treasure of the vocation to Religious Life will be no longer such a secret in our Church.

+ George Cantuar

Preface

The Religious Life evolved among Christians in the earliest centuries of the Church's existence. The pull to the desert for solitude in prayer, the desire to study the Scriptures, the impulse to a communal life, the desire to serve the society around in apostolic works - all worked for the emergence of communities of monks and nuns, brothers and sisters. This phenomenon spread to Britain with the Church itself and there was a range of monasteries and communities throughout the country by the Middle Ages.

At the time of the Reformation, Religious Communities sadly became an issue amidst the tragic conflicts and theological arguments that raged through Europe. In Britain, this was followed by the dissolution of all Religious houses and the apparent banishing of Religious Life from the Church of England. Yet through succeeding generations, the values and even practices of Religious Life found echoes in the life of university colleges, cathedrals, hospices and the care of the sick, alms houses, in the communal life found among families and also in some missionary movements. With the increasingly Catholic theology and ecclesiology of parts of the Church of England in the 1830s and 1840s, the idea of reviving the Religious Life gathered momentum and within the following decades many new communities were formed, with a variety of ministries and charisms, to stand alongside those of the Roman Catholic, Orthodox and other traditions within Christianity.

It is now over a hundred and fifty years since the revival of the Religious Life within the Church of England, and the communities have become accepted as part of the Church's life and history within the varied strands which make up the Anglican tradition. There are today over forty communities in the Church of England, with many more in other parts of the Anglican Communion.

In 1935, the Church set up the Archbishops' Advisory Council on the Relations of Bishops and Religious Communities, a body which gave official expression to the approval of Religious Life within the Church of England. Since that time, and particularly since the 1960s, Anglican Religious Communities have strengthened the links between themselves and also with communities in other Christian traditions. In order to encourage these links further and to witness to their way of life both within the Church and to those outside, the communities have produced this Year Book. It aims to be both a directory, and also to give some idea of their varied work and the contribution they make to the life of the Church.

Day of Prayer
for Vocations to the Religious Life

Setting a particular Sunday each year as a Day of Prayer for Vocations to the Religious Life was begun in 1992. This is currently **The Fifth Sunday after Trinity**, the collect for which is:

Almighty and everlasting God,
by whose Spirit
 the whole body of the Church
 is governed and sanctified:
hear our prayer
 which we offer for all your faithful people
that, in their vocation and ministry,
each may serve you in holiness and truth
 to the glory of your name;
through our Lord and Saviour Jesus Christ,
who is alive and reigns with you
in the unity of the Holy Spirit,
one God,
now and for ever. Amen.

Further information on the Day of Prayer may be obtained from
the Communities' Consultative Council, see page 16.

1 Community of All Hallows *at Ditchingham & Norwich*

 All Saints Sisters of the Poor *at Oxford & London; & in the USA*

 Society of the Precious Blood *at Burnham Abbey & Peterborough*

2 The Communities Consultative Council

3 Community of the Resurrection *at Mirfield & London; & in South Africa*

4 Community of Saint Francis & Society of Saint Francis *at Alnmouth, Birmingham, Brixton, Cambridge, Compton Durville, Edinburgh, Gladstone Park, Glasgow, Glasshampton, Hilfield, Newcastle-under-Lyme, Paddington, Plaistow & Stepney; & in Australia, New Zealand, Papua New Guinea, Solomon Islands & the USA*

 Society of the Franciscan Servants of Jesus & Mary *at Posbury*

5 Community of the Servants of the Will of God *at Crawley Down & Hove*

6 Community of the Epiphany *at Truro*

 Sisterhood of the Epiphany *at Ditchingham; & in India*

7 Community of the Holy Name in *Derby, Chester, Keswick, London, Nottingham & Oakham; & in Lesotho, South Africa & Swaziland*

8 Community of the Sisters of the Church *at Ham Common, Bristol, Clevedon, Little Weighton, Lytham St Annes &, Sudbury; & in Australia, Canada & Solomon Islands*

9 Community of St Denys *at Warminster, Barking & Salisbury*

10 Community of St Laurence *at Belper*

11 Order of St Benedict *at Alton Abbey, Burford Priory, Edgware Abbey, Elmore Abbey & Malling Abbey*

 Benedictine Community of the Holy Cross *at Rempstone*

 Community of the Holy Family *at Malling Abbey*

12 Our brothers & sisters living the Religious Life in other Communions of the Church

13 Community of the Glorious Ascension *at Kingsbridge*

14 Community of the Servants of the Cross *at Chichester*

 Society of the Sacred Cross *at Tymawr*

15 Community of St Mary the Virgin *at Wantage, Leeds, London, Smethwick, & in India & South Africa*

16 The Advisory Council for Religious Communities

in the Church, and today we pray for:

17 Our brothers & sisters living the Religious Life
in the wider Anglican Communion

18 Oratory of the Good Shepherd

19 Order of the Holy Paraclete *at Whitby, Dundee, Rievaulx, Leicester,
Wetherby & York; & in Ghana, South Africa & Swaziland*

20 Society of St Margaret *in Aberdeen, Chiswick, East Grinstead, Haggerston
& Walsingham; & in Haiti, Sri Lanka & the USA*

Ewell Monastery

21 Community of St Clare *at Freeland*

22 Community of the Sacred Passion *at Effingham, Camberwell, Norwich
& Walsall*

23 Society of the Holy Trinity *at Ascot Priory*

Society of Our Lady of the Isles *in the Shetland Isles*

24 Community of St John the Baptist *at Clewer; & in the USA*

Community of the Companions of Jesus the Good Shepherd *at Clewer*

Community of Reparation to Jesus in the Blessèd Sacrament *at Clewer*

25 Men and women testing their vocation as Novices

26 Sisters of the Love of God *at Oxford, Staplehurst & Hemel Hempstead;
& in New Zealand*

27 Community of St John the Divine *in Birmingham*

Society of St John the Evangelist *in London, Oxford & Haywards Heath;
& in the USA*

Sisters of Charity *at Plympton & Sunderland; & in the USA*

28 Oblates & Tertiaries; Associates & Companions

29 Community of St Peter *at Woking*

Community of St Peter, Horbury

Society of the Sisters of Bethany *at Hindhead & Southsea*

Society of the Sacred Mission *in Milton Keynes, Durham & London;
& in Australia & South Africa*

30 Community of St Andrew *in West London*

31 Those considering testing their vocation in the Religious Life,
particularly those serving a postulancy

News
of
Anglican
Religious
Life

Religious at Lambeth 1998

At the invitation of the Archbishop of Canterbury, members of Religious Communities are to be part of a chaplaincy team at the Lambeth Conference in 1998, under the Rt Revd Roger Herft, originally from Sri Lanka but at present the Bishop of Newcastle in New South Wales, Australia. The ten-yearly conference of Bishops of the Anglican Communion will be held from 18 July to 9 August 1998 at the University of Kent campus in Canterbury. The international group of Religious will begin praying there from 14 July, its members being:

Brother **Alfred Boonkong** SSF - from Malaysia, currently living in Australia;

Brother **Anthony Michael** SSF - from the Caribbean, currently living in the USA;

Sister **Catherine** SHC - from Korea;

Sister **Carol** CHN - from Derby, currently living at Lee Abbey in Devon;

Brother **Martin Smith** SSJE - the superior of SSJE in the USA;

Sister **Pamela** CAH - from Ditchingham, who will act as sacristan to the conference;

Sister **Rosina Ampah** OSH - from Ghana, currently living in the USA;

Brother **Samuel** SSF - Guardian of Hilfield Friary in Dorset.

During the conference, the team will be based at the centre of the university campus in the Senate House. This will be where the Religious say the Office and hold a Bible study every morning. A large octagonal room, upstairs in the Senate house, will be a place of silent prayer, with the sacrament reserved. Downstairs, another quiet room will house an exhibition of icons. The Religious will be joined each day by six people from the Canterbury area.

Special events in which the chaplaincy team will be involved are an overnight vigil (30-31 July), including a fast until the morning Eucharist, and three candle-lit pilgrimages (29 July, 3 August and 7 August). However, the underlying rôle of the group of Religious throughout the conference is the threefold task of hospitality, attentiveness to events and people, and being a worshipping community.

Symbol of the Anglican Communion

A Hundred & Fifty Years of Life

The Community of St John the Divine in Birmingham will celebrate their one hundred and fiftieth birthday in 1998. To mark this event, a special service of thanksgiving in Birmingham Cathedral is planned, which will take place on 11 July 1998. It will take the form of a Festal Eucharist at 12 noon and the preacher will be Bishop Hugh Montefiore. After the service, there will be a finger buffet. Members of Religious Communities and friends are warmly invited to attend.

The Community of St Mary the Virgin will also celebrate its one hundred and fiftieth anniversary in 1998, whilst two more communities celebrate their foundation centenaries. One is the Community of the Holy Family, now resident at West Malling Abbey, and the other is the Community of the Transfiguration in the USA.

Icon Panels go to Hove

The Fellowship of St Alban and St Sergius has recently loaned some vivid icon panels to the Community of the Servants of the Will of God. These have been hung on the walls of the chapel of the Monastery of Christ the Saviour, Hove. Painted in 1947 by Sr Joanna, a Russian nun, they were formerly in the Fellowship's headquarters in Ladbrooke Grove in London. The lower level comprises regional groups of saints and the upper level has scenes from the book of Revelation. As Father Gregory CSWG writes, 'They are remarkably suitable for the urban priority area of Hove.'

Building in Walsingham

When the Priory of Our Lady of Walsingham returned to being an autonomous house of the Society of St Margaret in January 1993, the noviciate was re-opened after a gap of several years. Without sufficient bedrooms for those wishing to test their vocation to the Religious Life, the Sisters decided to step out in faith and add an extension to the Priory. This was a tremendous task as the bank balance provided only for current needs. An appeal was opened and money began to be received.

By 1996, the long-awaited work received a severe set-back. Water was found under the entire building with devastating results, as the draining and underpinning would involve a total reconstruction of the ground floor. Costs would therefore far exceed the original estimate. Undaunted, the Community decided to re-launch the appeal at a more professional level and to go ahead.

The Sisters moved out of the Priory immediately after Easter 1997 and, following the renovations, moved back in February 1998. The Sisters are now able to welcome guests and private retreatants to the Priory. There is a plan to enlarge and improve the small cottage in the garden to increase such facilities. Major work on the chapel is also to be done as soon as there is sufficient funding available. The Sisters have so far raised about two-thirds of the money required for the whole project. So there is still a long way to go!

Golden Tertiaries

On 29 June 1998, the Tertiaries of the Order of the Holy Paraclete will celebrate the Golden Jubilee of their foundation. The Tertiary Order was officially recognized on St Peter's Day 1948 and arose from the initiative of Charlotte Houlden, a long-time friend of OHP. When she retired in 1946 from her work as a doctor in India, she went to live in Whitby at St Francis House, near the convent. She devised a Rule of Life, based on the OHP Rule, suitable for lay people in many walks of life, and others joined her in this commitment.

Since Sister Charlotte's death in 1956, several OHP sisters have had care of the Tertiaries, most notably Sister Mary Nina who was their Warden from 1962 to 1988. The Tertiary Order has flourished, not only in the UK but also particularly in South Africa. The growth in numbers includes members in Germany, New Zealand, Norway, Canada and the USA. As the Tertiary Order is open to Christians of any Trinitarian denomination, it has some members from the Methodist and URC churches.

Augustine Morris OSB
1905-97

O ne of the best known and loved of Anglican Religious, Dom Augustine Morris of Elmore Abbey, died on 20 January 1997 at the age of 91. His long monastic life, of more than seventy years included over twenty-five years as abbot of his own

Benedictine community. In many different ways, he also served both the Church and the Religious Life outside his monastery, and can be judged one of the most influential of Anglican Religious of the twentieth century.

Born David Freestone Morris on 19 August 1905 in Hammersmith, Augustine's family originated from Wales. His father died the following year and his widowed mother struggled bravely to bring him up on her own. Augustine went to Christ's Hospital school at Horsham, and in 1923, aged eighteen, he entered the Benedictine community at Pershore. He was professed on 1 November 1924. Within two years, the community had moved to Nashdom Abbey, where his commitment and abilities brought him appointment as prior in 1945 and election as abbot in 1948, a position he held until his resignation in 1974. He had been ordained priest in 1937. He was widely sought as a preacher and spiritual adviser.

Augustine was a significant influence on his community, but his influence stretched far beyond. He acted as warden to many women's communities and was regularly consulted by the leaders of other men's communities. For many Anglican Religious, Augustine's word came to be seen as the ultimate authority on the Religious Life. He played a prominent rôle on the Advisory Council throughout his Abbacy. Created in 1935, the Council had evolved as the main meeting-place for the superiors of the men's communities. In time, Augustine became one of the prime advocates of admitting women superiors to the Council, an aim in which he was eventually successful.

In ecumenical relations, Abbot Augustine was notable as the first Anglican Abbot to be invited to a Roman Catholic Benedictine Abbots' Congress. That was in 1967 and he was the only non-Roman Catholic observer present. This opened the way

6

for others, as well as himself, to attend subsequent congresses. His concern for unity was a life-long commitment, which began particularly after his meeting Abbé Paul Couturier in the 1930s.

For those who had the privilege to know him, however, his achievements in building up Religious Life in the Church of England and in ecumenical endeavours - impressive though they were - will not be what first comes to mind when they remember him. What they will recall will be his warmth and his humour, his concern for others and his ability to reach out to so many people. Friendship was sacred to Augustine and it is as a friend that so many who loved him will treasure his memory.

Loughborough Echo

Platinum Jubilee

In June 1841, Marian Rebecca Hughes became the very first woman to take vows in the Church of England since the Reformation. In 1911, she celebrated the seventieth (platinum) anniversary of those vows, dying the following year aged 95. Since then, a handful of Anglican Religious have lived to celebrate their platinum jubilees, including Sr Clare CSL (died 1961), Sr Lisette ASSP (died 1979), Sr Damaris ASSP (died 1985), Sr Ida CSD (died 1989), Sr Mary Francis CSF (died 1993) and Dom Augustine Morris OSB (died 1997).

On 21 January 1997, the day after Dom Augustine's death, Sr Mary Philomena of the Community of the Holy Cross at Rempstone joined this select group and became her own community's first platinum jubilarian.The photograph shows her with Mother Mary Luke, Sr Mary Michael and Sr Mary Julian. At the back is the Revd John Smith who, on the anniversary day, conducted a Communion Service according to the Book of Common Prayer. Despite her poor health, she appeared interested and alert and seemed to appreciate the significance of the occasion.

Sr Mary Philomena celebrated her 97th birthday on 10 August 1997. She died suddenly and unexpectedly the following 10 October, more than 76 years since she had first entered the CHC noviciate.

Speak the truth, yet giving courage, so that others feel you are on their side.

Donald Nicholl

Working with the Lonely

Mother Sheila CAH writes:

The Community of All Hallows, until recently, used to run St Anne's House, Ditchingham, as a small residential home. This regrettably became less viable and, after some heart-searching, the decision was made to transfer all residents and staff, who felt willing and able, to Adele House, the Community's nursing home in Bungay. This left St Anne's without a tenant.

The Community had an informal connection with the St Matthew Society. This is a Housing Association which operates as a Christian-based society within six counties in the east of England. The Society, as its policy document states, aims 'to develop small permanent homes where people from lonely backgrounds are able to live together as "small family groups". A degree of unintrusive support and spiritual help is available and residents are encouraged to enter the life of the neighbourhood and wider community.'

St Anne's House fitted admirably the Society's need for a house in the area, so negotiations were opened. Innumerable telephone calls, visits and letters followed, as well as (understandably enough) vociferous protests from some neighbours who at first felt threatened by such an unknown quantity. It was an act of faith on all our parts to 'press on bravely', as the words of an illuminated text in our Convent passage urged us! We entered a jungle of legalities presented by the drafting of a leasehold agreement to suit both parties – and their solicitors.

The house opened – unofficially – in 1996. It was a great joy to be present with the most important people (the residents), as well as what looked like half the village, for the official opening in July 1997. It is a project which the Community feels would be dear to our Foundress's heart, since there has always been room for the homeless and unwanted in the Community's vast umbrella. We continue to pray for them and with them, and to share a little of the administration as members of the Voluntary Committee which plays a vital part in the function of each house.

CHF moves to West Malling

Abbess Mary John OSB of the Abbey at West Malling writes:

It has been our privilege in 1997 to welcome the three remaining Sisters of the Community of the Holy Family from Baldslow to live in the Abbey Gate House, where they continue the round of Offices in the fifteenth-century Pilgrims' Chapel. Our two communities retain separate identities, but together we try to maintain the life of prayer in this ancient place.

The Holy Spirit breaks idols and securities because otherwise we will die in our security.
Donald Nicholl

One Hundred Not Out

Congratulations to three Anglican Religious who celebrated their one hundredth birthdays in 1997: Sr Pauline ASSP, Sr Jennetta CSD and Sr Mary Sethrid CHN. They join Sr Dorothy CSP (Woking) who reached the same age in 1996. The longest-lived Anglican Religious known to the editors was Sr Ida CSD, who died in 1989 aged 107.

Relaunching St Columba's

The Community of St Peter, at Woking, has decided to refurbish and relaunch its Retreat and Conference House (St Columba's) for 1998. The Community wishes to continue its nursing and care work, but expects to move towards the administration of this being done by professional lay workers. The Sisters hope to continue alongside in a pastoral rôle.

Zithers

When Father Philip Gaisford OSB, from Worth Abbey and co-ordinator of the Panel of Monastic Musicians, visited the Society of the Precious Blood at Burnham Abbey to talk about the Office, he also introduced the sisters to the use of the zither. This is an instrument with flowing, harp-like tones, and with a versatility which makes it a good accompaniment for chant. Through him, a member of the lay community at Worth, Michaela Morris, subsequently came to give introductory tuition on the instrument and generously lent SPB a zither for a few months, so that the sisters could experiment.

The experiment proved a great success, with the community both at Burnham Abbey and at St Pega's Hermitage, feeling that the psalms came alive in a new way with the resonances of this instrumental accompaniment. As a consequence, zithers were bought for both houses and their sound has become a regular feature of the community's worship.

Credit Unions

Debt is a global issue but is also on our own doorsteps. An article in this Year Book describes the campaign of Jubilee 2000, which aims at the cancelling of unrepayable world debt at an international level. On a local level, some Anglican Religious Communities are involved in supporting, by prayer and action, organisations which encourage Credit Unions.

One example would be in Wales, which is at present one of the poorest countries in the European Community. The Church in Wales has been invited to 'confront, understand and reflect on debt'. Christians, along with people from secular organizations, are doing this through Credit unions. These are mainly run by trained volunteers, with members able to save small amounts weekly. They are then able to take out loans at a rate of just 12%. Credit Unions encourage a saving habit, and therefore play a preventative rôle against debt and also keep money within the local community. They are an alternative banking system. For further information on Credit Unions, readers can contact: ABCUL, Holyoake House, Hanover Street, Manchester M60 0AS.

New Leaders

Several communities have had elections for new leaders during 1997-98. Brother Daniel succeeded Brother Brian as Minister General of the Society of St Francis on 1 July 1997. Brother Colin Wilfred was elected in turn to succeed Daniel as Minister Provincial of the Society's Australia/New Zealand Province. The sisters of the Community of St Mary the Virgin, Wantage, elected Mother Barbara Claire to succeed Mother Allyne in December 1997 and, two months later, Mother Anita took over leadership of the Sisters of the Church from Mother Judith. Two elections took place in January 1998. Sister Elizabeth Mary was elected to lead the Society of the Precious Blood, in place of Sister Margaret Mary, and the new Superior of the Community of the Resurrection is Father Crispin Harrison, who succeeds Father Silvanus Berry.

Listening for the Future

Mother Gillian Mary SSC writes:

During 1997-8, the Society of the Sacred Cross at Tymawr in Wales has been engaged in a 'Listening Year' with its Oblates, Companions, Associates and 'Alongsiders'. We are looking together towards the future. A 'listening group', consisting of five sisters and the Warden SSC, met with representatives of the extended family and then prepared a questionnaire for all committed to the Society and organised regional meetings. All findings were discussed and the listening group also met for a weekend's retreat before the Open Day in November, which brought us together with the Visitor, Bishop Rowan Williams. Recommendations from the listening group will be made to the SSC Chapter in 1998 for decision. It has been a blessed and encouraging experience for all concerned and we are thankful for the on-going commitment of our extended family.

Pilgrimage

The 1400th anniversary of the arrival in Britain of St Augustine of Canterbury was celebrated by many by going on pilgrimage. Anglican Religious were involved in many of the activities, most notably the singing of Solemn Monastic Vespers in Latin in Canterbury Cathedral by three hundred monks and nuns on 27 May 1997. The procession, winding around the cloisters, from the crypt to the nave took twenty-five minutes, and was witnessed by a large crowd both inside and outside the Cathedral. The Gregorian chant added to this moving ecumenical occasion, which ended with blessings from the Archbishop of Canterbury and Cardinal Hume.

Loughborough Echo

Whilst such gatherings won much publicity, other pilgrimages on a smaller scale were equally moving. The Community of the Holy Cross at Rempstone marked their 140th anniversary by combining it with a local parish pilgrimage. Participants walked from East Leake to Holy Cross Convent and the rain cleared sufficiently for an outdoor service on the convent lawn at which Mother Mary Luke preached.

In the anniversary year, two CHC sisters also were pleased to be invited to St Peter's, London Docks, the parish in which the community was founded, to attend the St Peter's day celebrations. Although CHC sisters had not worked in this area since 1933, there were still a few parishioners who could remember the branch house.

Donald Nicholl RIP

a Friend of Anglican Communities

Donald Nicholl died on 3 May 1997 in his 74th year. A Roman Catholic layman, Donald felt a call to offer his ministry particularly to women Religious and many Anglican Communities have reason to be grateful for his encouragement and wisdom. From a working-class background in Halifax, Donald became a lecturer in history, teaching in Edinburgh, at Keele University (where he became a Professor), and then in California. In 1981, he became director of the Ecumenical Institute at Tantur, near Jerusalem, a post he held for four years and where his long-standing ecumenical outlook brought him involvement in Inter-Faith relations. Perhaps his best-known book is* Holiness, *published in 1981. Here, Mother Gillian Mary SSC, from Tymawr Convent in Monmouthshire, offers some of her thoughts about him.*

Donald Nicholl (1923-97), historian and theologian and 'one of the outstanding Catholic laymen of his generation' was a good and challenging friend to many Anglican Religious Communities. He was a 'Pennine village lad', as he sometimes described himself, and his parents were loyal Anglicans. 'The moral soundness of that working-class Yorkshire Anglicanism, neither high nor low, but certainly Labour supporting, remained the ground beneath his feet all his life long.' (*The Tablet*, 10 May 1997). Donald was a brilliant historian, 'increasingly concerned with spiritual rather than material truth' (*The Daily Telegraph*, 20 May 1997) and among the fruits of that quest were his books: *Holiness* (1981), *The Testing of Hearts* (1989), *Triumphs of the Spirit in Russia* (1997) and *The Beatitude of Truth* (1997). All of them testify to that benevolent 'gazing' of which he often spoke. When asked during his last months what message he had for his friends in Religious Communities, he said simply 'Follow Jesus'. That message was the heart of his ministry and he was 'much in demand as a Conductor of Retreats, particularly for Anglican

Communities' (*The Times*, 17 May 1997).

The invitation to that ministry arose during a time of discernment without outside engagements; the Holy Spirit told him to respond to women Religious. (He had hoped the Holy Spirit would say 'walk on the moors', or 'enjoy rugby'!) Respond he did, to many Anglican communities, as we recalled with gratitude at the 1997 meeting of leaders. Many he did not visit in person were still touched by him, being immeasurably enriched by his books and writings.

When he came in person, his preparation was thorough and perceptive. He wrote to one Anglican community: 'What do you fear most? What gives you most delight? If you had the choice, which two changes would you make in your life? I expect my reason for suggesting this arises from my feeling with many communities that they are not 'coming clean' – not so much to me but with themselves. Peace and love, Donald.'

Gleanings from his talks were rich gatherings like Ruth's from the fields of Boaz and some of them are scattered through this Year Book. In his last year, his words were recorded. He said, 'The thoughts of a serene man are themselves prayer' and, on another occasion, 'My horizon – not death but Jesus resurrected, bearing the wounds of his crucifixion, now reigning in Heaven, having endowed us with his Spirit' (20 January 1997).

He knew himself to be at one in the Spirit with 'all who try and have tried and will try, as I myself do, however weakly, to live by the Spirit. All such people, from our earliest ancestors till the very last human being on this earth dwell in the same world, breathe the same Spirit. I am one in the Spirit with all of these. They and I are contemporaries. We belong to the same world, whether we are alive now on earth or dead or yet to be born' (6 March 1997).

Donald lived his prayer, his communion with God, his commitment to justice and peace. In the early morning, before it was light, he would leave the house to walk in the countryside. On the first visit to Tymawr, not knowing the place well, he fell down four steps onto the tarmac drive. His guardian angel must have been there for he was unhurt.

As a community, we pray for him and for Dorothy with affection. His perceptive comments still come to mind. He was a compassionate critic. To one of us, he sent this message on a Christmas card:

'Yesterday afternoon, as I was walking through the countryside, your face came up before me very vividly – not for the first time. You are very dear to me. With our love, Donald and Dorothy.'

In his 'fallow' periods, in his joy and depression, in his caring and his being cared for, in his patience and benevolent gazing, he pointed to the One he loved and served. He rests in peace. He prays for us as we do for him. We give thanks for him and rejoice in his resurrection.

Organisations

Advisory Council on the Relations of Bishops & Religious Communities
Commonly called 'The Advisory Council'

Created in 1935, the Advisory Council is responsible to the Archbishops and the House of Bishops for:
1 Advising the Bishops on:
   a) Questions arising about the charters and Rules of existing communities;
   b) The establishment of new communities;
   c) Matters referred to it by any Diocesan Bishop.
2 Advising existing communities and their Visitors on any matters they refer to it.
3 Giving guidance to those who wish to form communities.

The Council consists of at least thirteen members, of whom three are nominated by the Bishops and ten elected by the communities. Up to another five members may be co-opted. The Council is chaired by a diocesan Bishop appointed by the Archbishops of Canterbury and York.

Chairman: Rt Revd **David Smith**, Bishop of Bradford

House of Bishops' nominees:
Rt Revd & Rt Hon David Hope, Archbishop of York
Rt Revd Richard Harries, Bishop of Oxford
Rt Revd John Finney, Bishop of Pontefract

Communities' elected representatives:

Sister Alison OHP

Mother Jean Mary CHN

Abbot Basil Matthews OSB

Sister Lillian CSA

Father Christopher Lowe CR

Sister Margaret Angela CSJD

Brother Damian SSF

Sister Pamela CAH

Father Gregory CSWG

Sister Tessa SLG

Co-opted member:
Sister Elizabeth Mary CSD

Roman Catholic Observer:
Father Anthony Maggs CRL

Pastoral Secretary: Revd David Platt

Administrative Secretary: Miss Jane Melrose
Church House, Great Smith Street, London SW1P 3NZ
Tel: 0171 340 0212

The General Synod of the Church of England

Representatives of Lay Religious, Province of Canterbury

Sr Hilary CSMV
Chapter House
20 Dean's Yard
London
SW1P 3PA
Tel: 0171 222 5152; Fax: 0171 233 2072

Professed: 1954
Elected: 1995

Br Tristam SSF
The Friary of St Francis
Hilfield
Dorchester
Dorset DT2 7BE
Tel: 01300 341160; Fax: 01300 341293

Professed: 1971
Elected: 1994, re-elected: 1995

Representative of Ordained Religious, Province of Canterbury
Revd Sr Teresa CSA
St Andrew's House
2 Tavistock Road
Westbourne Park
London W11 1BA
Tel: 0171 229 2662; Fax: 0171 792 5993

Life Professed: 1975
Elected: 1995

Representative of Lay Religious, Province of York
Sr Margaret Shirley OHP
St Oswald's Pastoral Centre
Woodlands Drive
Sleights
Whitby YO21 1RY
Tel: 01947 810496

Professed: 1962
Elected: 1990, re-elected: 1995

Representative of Ordained Religious, Province of York
Fr Aidan Mayoss CR
House of the Resurrection
Mirfield
West Yorkshire WF14 0BN
Tel: 01924 494318; Fax: 01924 492738

Professed: 1964
Elected: 1993, re-elected: 1995

Conference of the Leaders of Anglican Religious Communities (CLARC)

The Conference meets in full once a year, usually in June. The addresses of the Leaders are listed under the appropriate community in the Directory of Communities *(see page 19 ff.)*.

Steering Committee

Mother Ann Verena CJGS
Mother Christine CSJD
Sr Elizabeth SSM
Mother Gillian Mary SSC

Mother Jean Mary CHN
Sr Joyce CSF
Mother Robina CSPH
Mother Sheila CAH

Communities' Consultative Council (CCC)

The Communities' Consultative Council was set up in 1975 and consists of elected representatives from Anglican Religious Communities in England. It exists to promote co-operation and the exchange of ideas between communities and also to provide general and vocational information about communities and Religious Life. The Council has an annual conference each September with the steering committee meeting on other occasions during the year.

Steering Committee

Revd Sr Elizabeth Mary CSD *(Chair)*
Church Flat, St Margaret's Centre, The Broadway, Barking, Essex IG11 8AS
Tel: 0181 594 1736 (evenings only)

Sr Aileen CSC *(Vice-Chair)*
Br Austin SSF *(Vice-Chair)*
Dom Bruce de Walt OSB
Sr Catherine CSC
Sr Clare SLG
Sr Elizabeth Anne CSMV

Br Harry SSF
Sr Margaret Anne ASSP
Sr Mary Stephen CSJB
Sr Rhonda CAH
Br Steven SSM

Mother Donella CSA *(Representative of CLARC)*
Sr Anne Griffiths OSU *(co-opted legal adviser)*

Conference of Religious
(CoR)

The Conference of Religious is open to all Roman Catholic Provincial leaders of Religious Congregations in England and Wales. The leaders of Anglican communities may be Associate members, which, apart from voting rights, means they receive all the same benefits and information as the Roman Catholic leaders.

CoR is run by an executive committee, elected from its members, which meets every two months. It deals with matters affecting men and women Religious, and various matters of interest to them. There is particular emphasis on peace and justice issues. Members of the executive also plan the day General Meeting in September and the residential Annual General Meeting and Conference held in Swanwick, Derbyshire, in January as well as representing the members on various associations and bodies. The secretarial staff deal with the administration and produce a monthly mailing full of useful information.

General Secretary of CoR:
Sr Gabriel Robin CSA
CoR Secretariat
114 Mount Street
London
W1Y 6AH
Tel: 0171 493 1817
Fax: 0171 409 2321
E-Mail: confrelig@aol.com

The Anglican representative on the CoR Executive Committee:
Sr Elizabeth Crawford SSM
St Saviour's Priory
18 Queensbridge Road
Haggerston
London
E2 8NS
Tel: 0171 739 6775

The CoR representative at CLARC:
Fr Anthony Maggs CRL
Christ Church Priory
229 High Street
London
SE9 1TX
Tel: 0181 850 1666

Care & Housing of Elderly Religious Project(CHERP)

The aims of CHERP are to enable Religious to make the best possible provision for the care of their elderly, sick and infirm members. This is done by the operation of a helpline, the organisation of conferences on matters of common concern, encouraging joint ventures between communities and other organisations, liaison with administrators and health authorities, and co-operation with nursing and hospital management bodies. The project was set up under the aegis of CoR, the Association of British Contemplatives and the Anglican Leaders' Conference. It publishes a Newsletter three times a year, in February, July and November, in order to disseminate information.

Project Co-ordinator:
Sr Velda Lake RSCJ
CHERP Office
3 Bute Gardens
London
W6 7DR
Tel: 0181 846 9681

Anglican Representative:
Abbess Mary Thérèse Zelent OSB
St Mary at the Cross
Priory Field Drive, Hale Lane
Edgware
Middlesex HA8 9PZ
Tel: 0181 958 7868

Association of British Contemplatives

The Association of British Contemplatives (ABC) is constituted by the women's contemplative communities of England, Scotland and Wales, Roman Catholic and Anglican. The purpose of the Association is: To foster solidarity and mutual co-operation between all the women's contemplative communities. To co-ordinate, if and when desired, initiatives and projects of mutual concern. To strengthen contemplative vision and values in the Church. To provide a structure for responding to current issues of concern To provide a channel of communication with the various Hierarchies and other official bodies.

The ABC Executive:
Abbess Joanna Jamieson OSB *(Chair)*
    Stanbrook Abbey, Callow End, Worcester WR2 4TD
Mother Mary of St Michael ODC *(Deputy Chair)*
    Carmelite Monastery of St Joseph, Waterside Rd, Kirkintilloch, Glasgow G66 3PE
Mother Rosemary SLG *(Anglican Representative)*
    Convent of the Incarnation, Fairacres, Oxford, OX4 1TB
Mother Aelred Casey OSC
    Monastery of Poor Clares, Cross Bush, Arundel, West Sussex BN18 9PJ
Sister Christina SA *(Treasurer)*, 17 Glisson Road, Cambridge CB1 2HA

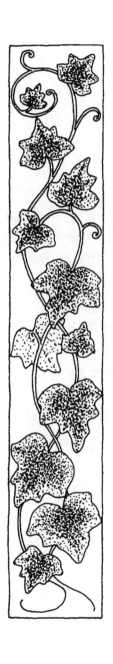

Directory
of
Communities

This Directory contains entries for almost all the Anglican Religious Communities in the United Kingdom, with addresses for many more communities worldwide.

Most communities have listed their members (either in profession order or alphabetically) and have provided information, where appropriate, on their guest accommodation, publications and the services and crafts they have for sale.

The Community of All Hallows

CAH

Founded 1855

All Hallows Convent
Belsey Bridge Road
Ditchingham
Bungay
Suffolk
NR35 2 DT

Tel: 01986 892749
Fax: 01986 892731

There is no typical All Hallows sister: we are as diverse in gifts and personality as are the Saints under whose patronage we try to live out the life to which God has called us. Central to the life of the Community is the daily Eucharist, the Divine Office and time for private prayer, meditation and spiritual reading.

The desire 'to serve Christ in one another and love as He loves us' overflows into the active life of the Community; into the welcome given to the many visitors to our three Guest Houses and our two Retreat and Conference Centres where Sisters are involved in the ministries of hospitality, spiritual direction and retreat giving.

The Community also cares for those with other needs – the very young at our day nursery and the elderly at our nursing/residential home. Our hospital is a special place for those needing to convalesce or having respite care, for day care, those needing physiotherapy and also for those nearing the end of their earthly pilgrimage. There is also a very loving concern and care for those who suffer from AIDS.

At Little Portion, Norwich, the community is working, in conjunction with the Social Services, to provide a centre for Family Contact days, where children and separated parents can be reunited for a few hours in a safe, welcoming ambience. There is space for 'halfway' accommodation in flats adjoining the house, and beds available too for emergency short-term residence and, occasionally, for ex-residents who may sometimes feel the need to 'come home' for a brief spell. We are also currently involved in a varied pastoral ministry in the Cathedral and beyond.

All enquiries about the life and work of CAH should be directed in the first place to the Reverend Mother CAH at the Convent.

MOTHER SHEILA
(Reverend Mother, elected Jun 1995)

The following all share the same address as All Hallows Convent:

St Gabriel's Conference and Retreat House
Tel: 01986 892133 (staff)
01986 895765 (residents)

Holy Cross Guest House
Tel: 01986 894092

St Michael's Retreat Centre
Tel: 01986 895749 (staff)
01986 894607 (residents)

All Hallows Guest House
Tel: 01986 892840

St Mary's Lodge *(House of silence & retreat)*
Tel: 01986 892731

* * *

Little Portion	All Hallows Hospital
Cross Lane	Station Road
Norwich NR3 1BU	Ditchingham
Tel: 01603 628087	Bungay
	Suffolk NR35 2QW
	Tel: 01986 892728

Community Publication
A newsletter is circulated yearly at All Saints tide. To be included on the mailing list, please write to All Hallows Convent at the address above.

Community History
Sister Violet CAH, *All Hallows, Ditchingham*, Becket Publications, Oxford, 1983.

Guest and Retreat Facilities
Enquiries about booking for the Retreat/Conference Centres should be addressed to the Convent Secretary at the Convent. Enquiries about staying at one of our guest houses should be addressed to the sister-in-charge of the relevant house.

St Gabriel's Centre, Ditchingham

Community of the Companions of Jesus the Good Shepherd

In 1996, the Community moved from its Mother House in Devon to live and work alongside the Community of St John the Baptist, while retaining its own ethos. The Community aims 'to express in service for others, Christ's loving care for his flock.' At present, this service includes involvement in lay and local non-stipendiary ministry training, offering companionship to those seeking to grow in the spiritual life through spiritual direction, quiet days and retreats, and especially the befriending of the elderly, lonely and those in need.

CJGS

Founded 1920

*Convent of St John the Baptist
Hatch Lane, Clewer
Windsor, Berkshire
SL4 3QR*

Tel: 01753 850618

*Lauds
7.30 am*

*Tierce
9.00 am
(8.45 am Sun
& major feasts)*

*Eucharist
9.10 am
(9.00 am Sun
& major feasts)*

*Sext
12.00 noon*

*Vespers
5.30 pm*

*Compline
8.45 pm*

MOTHER ANN VERENA
(Mother Superior, assumed office 20 Mar 1996)

Sr Angela Felicity
Sr Freda *(at Fairacres)*
Sr Ena Florence *(at Croydon)*
Sr Evelyn Theresa
Sr Kathleen Frideswide
Sr Phyllis Mary *(at Exeter)*

Community Publication
CJGS News. Contact the Mother Superior.

Community Wares
Calligraphy, candles, church needlework.

Guest and Retreat Facilities
See the entry for the Community of St John the Baptist.

Associates
Associates of the Community are members of the Fellowship of St Augustine. They follow a rule of life drawn up with the help of one of the Sisters. They give support to the Community through their prayer, interest and alms, and are remembered in prayer by the Community. They and the Community say the 'Common Devotion' daily. They are truly our extended family.

Community of the Glorious Ascension

CGA

Founded 1960

*The Priory
Start Point
Kingsbridge
Devon TQ7 2NG*

*Tel & Fax:
01548 511474*

The Community aims to combine a life of prayer and worship with that of going out to support itself through daily work. The brothers generally live in small groups bound together in the corporate pattern of monastic life. The mission of the Community is primarily that of being with and amongst people in ordinary situations.

BR SIMON
(Prior, assumed office 20 May 1993)

Community Publication
CGA Newsletter, published annually. Write to the Prior.

Guest and Retreat Facilities
Since moving to Devon in 1996, the Community has been able to offer some hospitality to individuals and families. This is not a retreat facility, but a place with an opportunity for relaxation and reflection within a community environment. The Community welcomes individuals by day and can offer accommodation in twin-bedded en-suite rooms for short periods. The main house has two rooms which can accommodate ten people comfortably for gatherings and meetings. There are also cottages set in the converted barn, adjacent to the main house, which are fully self-contained. Each has a sitting room and a separate fully-equipped kitchen/dining area.

The Priory is set in six acres of land, largely hillside with areas developed as gardens, with small local beaches nearby. All visitors are welcome to make use of the grounds, and also the chapel and sitting room in the main house.

Benedictine Community of the Holy Cross, Rempstone

CHC

Founded 1857

Holy Cross Convent
Rempstone Hall
Nr Loughborough
LE12 6RG

(Southwell Diocese)

Tel: 01509 880336
Fax: 01509 881812

Matins
6.55 am

Lauds
7.30 am

Terce
9.00 am

Sext
11.45 am (12.10 Tue)

None
1.30 pm

Vespers
4.30 pm (4.00 pm Thu)

Compline
8.00 pm

Mass
12.00 noon (9.15 am Tue)

The Community of the Holy Cross was founded in 1857 by Elizabeth Neale (sister of John Mason Neale, the hymnographer), at the invitation of Father Charles Fuge Lowder. The foundation was intended for Mission work in Father Lowder's parish of London Docks, but succeeding generations felt that the Community was being called to a life of greater withdrawal, and earlier this century the Benedictine Office, and later the Rule of St Benedict, were adopted.

The Community aims to achieve the Benedictine balance of prayer, study and work. All the work, whether manual, artistic or intellectual, is done within the Enclosure. The daily celebrations of the Eucharist and the Divine Office are the centre and inspiration of all activity.

Apart from worship, prayer and intercession, and the work of maintaining the house, garden and grounds, the Community's works are: the publications and greetings cards described below; providing retreats and quiet days; and dealing with a large postal apostolate.

SR MARY LUKE WISE
(Mother Superior, elected 8 Nov 1991)
SR MARY JULIAN GOUGH (Assistant Superior)

Sr Mary Katharine Walsh
Sr Mary Michael Titherington
Sr Mary Bernadette Priddin
Sr Mary Laurence Bagshaw
Sr Mary Joseph Thorpe
Sr Mary Sylvia Driscall

Novices: 1

Obituary
10 Oct 1997   Sr Mary Philomena Blunt,
aged 97 years, professed 70 years

Community Publications
The sisters write and publish two sets of leaflets of devotional and spiritual content. One concerns *Unity between Christians* and a wider ecumenism. The other is on *Prayer and Faith*, reflecting the mission of the Church in the world. There is also an advent *Newsletter* published in early December. Both are available from the Publications Secretary.

Community History
Alan Russell,*The Community of the Holy Cross Haywards Heath 1857 - 1957: A Short History of its Life and Work,* 1957.

Community Wares
A great variety of prayer and greeting cards are available for sale. Some are produced by the sisters and others are from a number of different sources.

Guest and Retreat Facilities
There is limited accommodation for residential, private retreats: one small guest cottage in the grounds; main meals are taken at the Convent. The Community also provides for Quiet Days for individuals or groups up to twenty.

Oblates and Associates
The Community has women Oblates who are attached to it in a union of mutual prayers. Each has a rule of life adapted to her particular circumstances. Oblates are not Religious but they seek to live their life in the world according to the spirit of the Rule of St Benedict.
There are also Associates who have a much simpler rule.

The Community Chapel, Rempstone

Community of the Holy Family

CHF

Founded 1898

*The Gatehouse
St Mary's Abbey
West Malling, Kent
ME19 6LP*

Tel: 01732 849016

*Mattins
6.35 am (8.00 am Sun)*

*Eucharist
7.30 am (9.00 am Sun)*

*Terce
9.35 am (10.35 am Sun)*

*Midday Office
12.20 pm
(12.35 pm Sun)*

*Vespers
4.50 pm*

*Compline
7.50 pm*

In January 1997, the community moved from Baldslow to the Gatehouse of West Malling Abbey. It is anticipated that the spirit of the educational work begun by the Foundress, Mother Agnes Mason, at the beginning of this century, will still be continued in the eastern end of the Diocese of Chichester through the Mother Agnes Trust which undergirds the Community of the Holy Family. The charity in the future will seek to provide a theological library and an extensive educational resource centre.

MOTHER KATHLEEN MARY
(Mother Superior, assumed office 1992)

Sr Jean
Sr Phyllis Ella

The Norman Tower from the Gate House, Malling Abbey

Community of the Holy Name

CHN

Founded 1865

Convent of the Holy
Name
Morley Road
Oakwood
Derby
DE21 4QZ

Tel: 01332 671716

Prime
7.45 am   (8.15 am Tue)

Eucharist
8.00 am
(12.20 pm Tue & Thu)

Mattins
9.15 am
(8.45 am Thu,
9.30 am Sun)

Midday Office
12.45 pm
(12.05 pm Tue & Thu)

Vespers
5.00 pm

Compline
9.15 pm   (8.00 pm Sat)

The Sisters combine the life of prayer with service to others in their evangelistic and pastoral outreach and by maintaining their houses as centres of prayer where they can be available to others. They run a retreat house and conference centre in Chester, a small guest house in Derby, and are able to take one or two guests in the house at Keswick. In other houses, and from the Convent in Derby, the Sisters are involved in parish work, prison visiting, retreat-giving and work among some who are disabled, and those who come for counselling.

The houses in Southern Africa (see overseas addresses) are concerned with educational, evangelistic and creative work along with African workers, and itself being multi-racial, the Community is a witness against any form of racism. The members of the Fellowship of the Holy Name are an extension of its life and witness in the world.

MOTHER JEAN MARY
(Provincial Superior, assumed office 14 Jan 1994)
SR MONICA JANE *(Assistant Provincial Superior)*

Sr Barbara Mary	Sr Theresa Margaret
Sr Michael	Sr Mary Patricia
Sr Colette	Sr Beryl
Sr Mary Sethrid	Sr Lisbeth
Sr Christian	Sr Vivienne Joy
Sr Penelope	Sr Charity
Sr Judith	Sr Renate
Sr Ruth	Sr Elizabeth Clare
Sr Mary Janet	Sr Bernardine
Sr Mary Alison	Sr Vivienne
Sr Francesca Mary	Sr Diana
Sr Sheila Margaret	Sr Edith Margaret
Sr Nikola	Sr Dorothy
Sr Marjorie Jean	Sr Pauline Margaret
Sr Mariette	Sr Pamela
Sr Mary Ruth	Sr Dorothy Helen
Sr Barbara	Sr Carol
Sr Gladys Mary	Sr Pippa
Sr Joy	Sr Rosemary
Sr Elizabeth Rachel	Sr Irene
Sr Brenda	Sr Lynfa
Sr Verena	Sr Elaine Mary
Sr Constance	Sr Fiona Mary
Sr Lilias	Sr Julie Elizabeth
Sr Marjorie Eileen	
Sr Jessica Mary	*Novices: 3*

Society of the Holy Trinity: Sr Rosemary

Obituaries

1 Mar 1997	Sr Marjorie, aged 91 years, professed 37 years
4 Mar 1997	Sr Mary Ella, aged 88 years, professed 54 years
18 Sep 1997	Sr Rachel Christine, aged 75 years, professed 39 years
29 Dec 1997	Sr Felicity, aged 81 years, professed 48 years

The Retreat House
11 Abbey Square
Chester CH1 2HU
Tel: 01244 321801

Cottage 5
Lambeth Palace
London SE1 7JU
Tel: 0171 9285407

88 Braunston Road
Oakham
Rutland LE15 6LE
Tel: 01572 770287

St Michael's
53 Wimborne Road
Radford
Nottingham NG7 5PD
Tel: 0115 9785101

Holy Name House
Ambleside Road
Keswick
Cumbria CA12 4DD
Tel: 01768 772998

6 St Peter's Court
398 Woodborough Road
Nottingham NG3 4JF
Tel: 0115 9608794

Community History
History of the Community of the Holy Name, 1865 to 1950, published by CHN, 1950.

Community Wares
Candles, recycled cards and hand-painted cards, as well as prayer stones (either painted or with a Celtic design) are all for sale at the Convent (but not through the post).

Guest and Retreat Facilities
There are opportunities for individuals to make a private retreat at the guest house, and Sisters would be prepared to give help and guidance if requested. We do not organise group retreats.

Fellowship of the Holy Name
The Fellowship is comprised of ecumenically-minded Christians who feel called to share with the Community in their life of prayer and service.
   Members have a personal Rule of Life, which they have drawn up in consultation with a particular Sister. She will keep in contact and help with a regular review. This rule will include daily private prayer, regular prayer and worship with the local Christian community, as well as time and space for their own well-being and creativity. Each rule varies with the individual. A six-month probation living the rule is required before formal admission to the Fellowship. This usually takes place at the Convent in the context of the Eucharist. There are regional meetings for members living in the same area, and the Community distributes a quarterly magazine comprised of articles submitted by members.

Community of the Resurrection

The Community consists of priests and laymen living together as brothers a life devoted to prayer and worship, work and study. They undertake a wide range of pastoral ministry, both in the UK and South Africa. Their work includes a theological college at Mirfield and retreat houses, together with evangelism and counselling.

CR

Founded 1892

House of the Resurrection Mirfield West Yorkshire WF14 0BN

Tel: 01924 494318
Fax: 01924 490489

CRISPIN HARRISON
(assumed office 6 Jan 1998)
ANTONY GRANT *(Prior)*

Trevor Huddleston *(bishop)*
Benjamin Baynham
Dominic Whitnall
Luke Smith
Anselm Genders *(bishop)*
Roy France
Timothy Stanton
Aelred Stubbs
Vincent Girling
Kingston Erson
Clifford Green
Zachary Brammer
Benedict Green
Alexander Cox
Eric Simmons
Aidan Mayoss
Silvanus Berry

Robert Mercer *(bishop)*
Simon Holden
Christopher Lowe
Jonathan Critchley
Harry Williams
David Wilson
Nicolas Stebbing
John Gribben
Peter Allan
Andrew Norton
George Guiver
William Nicol
Philip Nichols
Thomas Seville
James Springett
Novices: 1
Postulants: 2

Obituary
1 Sep 1997 Damian Garwood, aged 65 years,
professed 28 years

St Michael's Priory
14 Burleigh Street
London WC2E 7PX
Tel: 0171 379 6669
Fax: 0171 240 5294

St Peter's Priory
PO Box 991
Southdale 2135
SOUTH AFRICA
Tel & Fax: +27 11 434 2504

Community Publication
CR Quarterly. Write to the Director FR at the House of the Resurrection.

Community History
Alan Wilkinson, *The Community of the Resurrection: A centenary history*, SCM Press, London, 1992.

Community Wares
Postcards of the House, leaflets on prayer: apply to Mirfield Publications at the House of the Resurrection.

Guest and Retreat Facilities
Retreats are listed in *Retreats* (formerly *Vision*).
HOUSE OF THE RESURRECTION: twenty single rooms, two double rooms.
Apply to the Guestmaster.

A further retreat house, owned but not staffed by CR, is:
ST FRANCIS' HOUSE, Hemingford Grey
Huntingdon, Cambs., PE18 9BJ
Tel: 01480 46218
Seventeen single rooms, three twin rooms. Apply to the Warden.

Mirfield Centre *Director:* Bridget Rees
The Centre co-ordinates the resources of the College of the Resurrection, the eastern wing of the Northern Ordination Course based at the Centre, and the Faith in Community Project, with the support of the Community of the Resurrection, so as to make them available to ecumenical partners locally in the West Yorkshire Ecumenical Council and beyond.

College of the Resurrection
Mirfield
West Yorkshire WF14 0BW
Tel: 01924 490441
Fax: 01924 492738

Faith in Community Project
The Mirfield Centre
Mirfield
West Yorkshire WF14 0BW
Tel: 01924 481911; Fax: 01924 492738

Fraternity of the Resurrection
The Fraternity is an integral part of the family of the Community of the Resurrection. There are four categories of membership:
1. OBLATES: priests and laymen who accept a vocation to live their lives according to the evangelical counsels of poverty, chastity and obedience.
2. COMPANIONS: men and women, clerical and lay, who are joined to the Community in a rule of worship, study and service.
3. ASSOCIATES: those who wish for a less demanding link with the Community, or who already have a comparable relationship with another Community.
4. FRIENDS: Christians or members of another Faith or of none who consider that while the obligations of Eucharistic worship are not for them, they are nevertheless interested in the Community.

Community of the Sacred Passion

CSP

Founded 1911

*The Convent of the
Sacred Passion
Lower Road
Effingham
Leatherhead
Surrey
KT24 5JP*

Tel: 01372 457091

*Morning Prayer
7.10 am*

*Mass
7.30 am
(Mon, Tue, Wed, Fri)*

*Prayer before noon
8.40 am*

*Midday Office
12.10 pm*

*Evening Prayer
6.00 pm*

*Compline
8.45 pm*

The Community was founded to serve Africa by a life of prayer and missionary work. Prayer is the centre of the life of the Community and all activity flows from it. The Mother House is now in England. The Community withdrew from Africa in 1991 leaving behind the Tanzanian Community of St Mary of Nazareth and Calvary, which they had founded. The Community of St Mary now has nine houses in Tanzania and one in Zambia (see overseas section).

The way the sisters live out their vocation depends on local circumstances. At Effingham, guests are welcomed for times of quiet and private retreat. Visiting the sick and house-bound and prison, cathedral and hospital chaplaincy work are also undertaken. Kennington and Walsall often have visitors. In these houses, sisters give help in the parishes which includes visiting, speaking, conducting retreats, hospital and industrial chaplaincy, and interfaith dialogue. A small group of sisters live next to the St Julian's Shrine in Norwich. Here, the main ministry is hospitality to visitors to the Shrine.

MOTHER GLORIA
(Mother Superior, assumed office 12 Sep 1989)
SR JACQUELINE *(Sister Superior)*

Sr Stella	Sr Ruby
Sr Rose Mary	Sr Joan Thérèse
Sr Greta	Sr Gillian Mary
Sr Felicitas	Sr Rhoda
Sr Blandina	Sr Mary Stella
Sr Olive Marian	Sr Angela
Sr Etheldreda	Sr Philippa
Sr Joanna Mary	Sr Joy
Sr Mary Columba	Sr Lucia
Sr Jean Margaret	Sr Mary Kathleen
Sr Dorothy	Sr Mary Margaret
Sr Thelma Mary	Sr Maureen
Sr Mary Joan	Sr Phoebe

Other UK Houses

The Convent
14 Laing House
Walstead Road
Walsall WS5 4NJ
Tel: 01922 644267

6 Calais Street
Camberwell
London SE5 9LP
Tel: 0171 274 0777

All Hallows House, St Julians's Alley, Rouen Rd,
Norwich NR1 1QT   *Tel: 01603 624738*

Community History
Sister Mary Stella CSP, *She Won't Say 'No': The history of the Community of the Sacred Passion,* privately published, 1984.

Guest and Retreat Facilities
Private retreatants are welcome in the small guest house at Effingham.

Oblates
These are men and women who feel called to associate themselves with the aims of the community, by prayer and service, and by a life under a Rule. They have their own Rule of Life which will vary according to their particular circumstances. The Oblates are helped and advised by the Mistress of Oblates.

Associates
These are men and women who share in the work of the community by prayer, almsgiving and service of some kind. They pray regularly for the community.

Priest Associates
They pray regularly for the community and offer Mass for it three times a year, of which one is Passion Sunday (the Sunday before Palm Sunday).

Friends
They pray regularly for the community and help it in any way they can.

All those connected with the community are prayed for daily by the Sisters and remembered by name on their birthdays. They receive the four monthly intercession paper.

The Lord
showed me a little thing
the size of a hazel nut,
in the palm of my hand
and it was round as a ball.
I looked upon it
with the eye of my understanding
and thought:
'What may this be?'
And it was answered thus:
'It is all that is made.'
For God made it, God loveth it
and God keepeth it.

Julian of Norwich

Community of St Andrew

CSA

Founded 1861

St Andrew's House
2 Tavistock Road
Westbourne Park
London
W11 1BA

Tel: 0171 229 2662

Full membership of the Community consists of Professed Sisters who are ordained, or who, though not seeking ordination, serve in other forms of diaconal ministry, such as the caring professions. The fundamental ministry is the offering of prayer and worship, evangelism, pastoral work and hospitality. This is carried out through parish and specialised ministry.

MOTHER DONELLA *(deacon)*
(Mother Superior, assumed office 13 Oct 1994)
SR DENZIL *(priest) (Assistant Superior)*

Sr Joan *(deacon)*	Sr Pamela *(deaconess)*
Sr Barbara *(deaconess)*	Sr Lillian *(deacon)*
Sr Hilary *(deacon)*	Sr Patricia *(deacon)*
Sr Eleanor *(deaconess)*	*(Novice Guardian)*
Sr Dorothy *(deaconess)*	Sr Teresa *(priest)*
Sr Julian *(priest)*	Sr Gerd *(deacon)*

Obituaries

9 May 1997   Sr Hildegard *(deaconess)*, aged 94 years, professed 55 years

27 Sep 1997   Sr Verity *(deaconess)*, aged 77 years, professed 43 years

Community Publication

Morning Prayer
7.30 am
7.10 am (Mon & Wed)
8.00 am (Sat)

St Andrew's Review & St Andrew's Newsletter (alternate years). Write to the Revd Mother CSA.

Guest and Retreat Facilities

Facilities for individual or group quiet days. One room for residential (individually-guided or private) retreat.

Eucharist
7.30 am (Mon & Wed)
9.30 am (Tue)
12.30 pm (Thu & Fri)

Associates

Our Associates are part of our extended Community family. They may be men, women, clergy or lay, and follow a simple Rule of Life, which includes praying for the Sisters and their work. Friends are also part of our fellowship of prayer and support the Sisters in many ways.

Midday Prayer
12.45 pm
1.15 pm (Sun)
12.15 pm (Thu & Fri)

The Sisters pray for the Associates and Friends every day and also arrange special retreats, quiet days, and social gatherings for them every year, and can be available to give help or guidance if required.

Evening Prayer
6.00 pm

Night Prayer
9.00 pm

Community of St Clare

OSC

Founded 1950

St Mary's Convent
178 Wroslyn Road
Freeland
Witney
Oxfordshire
OX8 8AJ

Tel: 01993 881225
Fax: 01993 882434

The Community of St Clare is part of the Society of St Francis. We are a group of women who live together needing each other's help to give our whole lives to the worship of God. Our service to the world is by our prayer, in which we are united with all people everywhere. We have a guest house so that others may join in our worship, and share the quiet and beauty with which we are surrounded. We try to provide for our own needs by growing much of our own food, and by our work of printing, wafer baking, writing and various crafts. This also helps us to have something material to share with those in greater need.

SR PAULA FORDHAM
(Abbess, elected 7 May 1997)
SR ALISON FRANCIS HAMILTON *(Deputy Leader)*

Sr Elsie Felicity Watts
Sr Patricia Wighton
Sr Gillian Clare Amies
Sr Brenda Michael Stephenson
Sr Mary Margaret Broomfield
Sr Susan Elisabeth Leslie
Sr Damian Davies
Sr Michaela Davis
Sr Mary Kathleen Kearns
Sr Elizabeth Farley
Novices: 2

Office of Readings
5.30 am

Morning Prayer
7.00 am

Eucharist
8.30 am

Midday Prayer
12.00 noon

Evening Prayer
5.00 pm

Night Prayer
8.15 pm

Community Wares
Printing, cards, crafts, altar breads.
Tel & Fax to Print Shop: 01993 882434

Guest and Retreat Facilities
Men, women and children are welcome at the guest house. It is not a 'silent house' but people can make private retreats if they wish. Please write to the Guest Sister at the Convent address.

Address of the Guest House (for guests arriving)
The Old Parsonage, 168 Wroslyn Road, Freeland
Oxford OX8 8AQ
Tel: 01993 881227

Community of St Denys

CSD

Founded 1879

*St Denys Retreat Centre
2/3 Church Street
Warminster
BA12 8PG*

*Tel: 01985 214824
(10 am - 12.00 noon,
6.45 pm - 8.00 pm)*

The Community was founded for mission work at home and overseas. At present the work includes parish work, missions and retreat work. Sisters also act as tutors for lay-training courses in the Salisbury Diocese and some as spiritual directors.

There are two houses in Warminster in addition to the Retreat House.

All enquiries should be sent c/o the Retreat Centre or to the Revd Mother in Salisbury.

REVD MOTHER FRANCES ANNE *(priest)*
(Mother Superior, assumed office 27 Jun 1987)

Sr Jennetta	Sr Christine
Sr Ruth	Sr Eileen
Sr Stephanie *(priest)*	Sr Margaret Mary
Sr Doris	Sr Phyllis
Sr Carol	Sr Elizabeth Mary *(priest)*
Sr Gladys	
Sr Julian	*Novices: 1*

Revd Mother CSD
Sarum College, 19 The Close, Salisbury SP1 2EE
Tel: 01722 339761

Church Flat, St Margaret's Centre, The Broadway
Barking, Essex IG11 8AS
Tel: 0181 594 1736 (evenings only)

Community Publication
Annual *Newsletter* and quarterly prayer leaflet. Write to the Secretary of the S. Denys Fellowship, 2/3 Church St, Warminster, Wilts BA12 8PG.

Community History
CSD: The Life & Work of St Denys', Warminster to 1979, published by CSD, 1979.

Guest and Retreat Facilities
ST DENYS RETREAT CENTRE (2/3 Church Street, Warminster, Wilts, BA12 8PG) is available for various types of retreat and parish conferences. Guests are also welcome.

The Sisters lead 'Walk-in to quietness with God' days, Individually-Guided Retreats and traditional preached Retreats, both in Warminster and elsewhere.

*Morning Prayer
7.15 am*

*Midday Prayer
12.30 pm*

*Evening Prayer
& Eucharist
5.00 pm*

*Compline
Time varies*

Community Wares
Recycled cards for charities.

Associates
CSD has oblates, associates (ordained and lay), and a fellowship (i.e. friends).
There have been resident oblates in the past, although there are none at present.

Sister Elizabeth Mary CSD, Mother Frances Anne CSD & Sister Stephanie CSD
at their ordination to the priesthood;
with Bishop Roger Sainsbury of Barking, Bishop David Stancliffe of Salisbury
and the Very Revd Hugh Dickinson, Dean of Salisbury
in Salisbury Cathedral on 9 October 1995

Community of St Francis

CSF

Founded 1905

This autonomous Community is part of the Society of St Francis: the First Order Sisters. Sisters are engaged in spiritual direction and evangelistic and caring ministry, sometimes alongside brothers of the Society. Some part-time salaried work is necessary to help generate income. Guests are received in all houses of the Community; in some, there is space for retreatants and other groups. A four-fold Office is offered using *The Daily Office SSF*, a version of *Celebrating Common Prayer*. The Eucharist is central to the Community's life and is celebrated regularly in all houses.

SR TERESA (4)
(Minister General, assumed office 7 Feb 1996)

European Province
SR JOYCE (2)
(Minister Provincial, assumed office 30 Jul 1996)

Sr Alison Mary (1)	Sr Jackie (3)
Sr Angela Helen (1)	Sr Jannafer (4)
Sr Angela Mary (1)	Sr Jennie (4)
Sr Barbara (1)	Sr Judith Ann (3)
Sr Chris (5)	Sr Moyra (3)
Sr Christine James (1)	Sr Nan (2)
Sr Elizabeth (1)	Sr Pat (3)
Sr Gabriel (3)	Sr Patricia Clare (4)
St Gina (5)	Sr Rose (2)
Sr Gwenfryd Mary (1)	Sr Veronica (1)
Sr Helen Julian (3)	
Sr Hilary (1)	*Novices:* 4

Listed alphabetically, with the house code beside each name.

Community of the Presentation: Sr May (1)

Obituary
27 Jul 1997   Sr Leonore, aged 88 years, professed 35 years

St Francis House (1) 113 Gillott Rd, Birmingham B16 0ET
Tel: 0121 454 8302; Fax 0121 455 9784

43 Endymion Road (2) Brixton, London SW2 2BU
Tel: 0181 671 9401

St Francis Convent (3) Compton Durville, South Petherton, Somerset, TA13 5ES
Tel: 01460 240473 & 241248; Fax: 01460 242360

Greystones St Francis (4) First Ave, Portill, Newcastle-under-Lyme, Staffs ST5 8QX
Tel: 01782 636839   *(Minister General, Tel & Fax: 01782 611180)*

10 Halcrow Street (5) Stepney, London E1 2EP   *Tel: 0171 247 6233*
(Minister Provincial, Tel & Fax: 0181 674 5344; E-Mail: Joycecsf@AOL.com)

New Zealand Region
SR MAUREEN *(Deputy Minister Provincial)*
Sr Fay   Sr Phyllis

33 Carlton Gore Road, Grafton, Auckland 1, NEW ZEALAND
Tel: +64 9 377 5054; Fax +64 9 377 5059

American Province
SR PAMELA CLARE *(Minister Provincial)*

Sr Catherine Joy	Sr Elizabeth Ann	Sr Ruth
Sr Cecilia	Sr Jean	*Novices:* 1

St Francis House, 3743 Cesar Chavez Street, San Francisco, CA 94110, USA
Tel: +1 415 824 0288;   Fax: +1 415 826 7569   E-Mail: csf@sfo.com

Community History
Elizabeth CSF, *Corn of Wheat*, Becket Publications, Oxford, 1981.

Community Publication
franciscan (published by SSF sisters and brothers), three times a year.
Write to The Editor SSF, The Friary, Hilfield, Dorchester, Dorset DT2 7BE.

Guest and Retreat Facilities
COMPTON DURVILLE   Guests are welcome, both men and women, in groups or as
individuals. There are fourteen single rooms and two twin-bedded. Day groups of
thirty can be accommodated. A programme is available from the Guest Sister.

Third Order
The Third Order of the Society of St Francis consists of men and women, ordained
and lay, married or single, who believe that God is calling them to live out their
Franciscan vocation in the world, living in their own homes and doing their own
jobs. Living under a rule of life, with the help of a spiritual director, members
(called tertiaries) encourage one another in living and witnessing to Christ, being
organised in Regions and Areas to enable regular meetings to be held. There are
some 1800 tertiaries in the European Province of this world-wide Order, with a
Minister General and five Ministers Provincial to cover the relevant Provinces.
Information about the Third Order (often called Tertiaries) can be obtained from:
The Minister Provincial TSSF, Lochside, Lochwinnoch, Renfrewshire PA12 4JH.

Companions
Companions are individual Christians who wish to associate themselves with the
Society through prayer, friendship and in seeking to live the spirit of the Gospel in
the way of St Francis. For more information about becoming a Companion contact:
The Secretary for Companions, Hilfield Friary, Dorchester, Dorset DT2 7BE.

Community of St John the Baptist

CSJB

Founded 1852

Convent of St John the
Baptist
Hatch Lane
Clewer
Windsor
Berkshire
SL4 3QR

Tel: 01753 850618

Lauds
7.30 am

Tierce
9.00 am
(8.45 am Sun & major
feasts)

Eucharist
9.10 am
(9.00 am Sun & major
feasts)

Sext
12.00 noon

Vespers
5.30 pm

Compline
8.45 pm

The Sisters' life of worship and service revolves around a daily Eucharist, a five-fold Office, and private prayer. Their works include the Clewer Spirituality Centre, which caters for both group and individual retreats and quiet days; for conferences and workshops. There is a guest wing and a Church Embroidery Room. St Anne's House is a home for the elderly and St John's Convent Home accommodates mentally handicapped women. The Sisters outside work includes parish work, missions and retreat giving. Individual Sisters are involved in the local Day centre, the Thames Valley Hospice and work with the deaf/blind; they take part in local prayer and study groups, and ecumenical projects. There is an affiliation in Mendham, New Jersey, USA (see overseas section).

MOTHER JANE OLIVE
(Reverend Mother Superior, installed 19 Aug 1992)
SR ZOE *(Assistant Superior)*

Sr Gladys Mary	Sr Monica
Sr Letitia	Sr Elizabeth Jane
Sr Marjorie	Sr Pamela
Sr Moira	Sr Veronica Joan
Sr Sheila	Sr Mary Stephen
Sr Doreen	Sr Anne
Sr Edna Frances	

Community of Reparation to Jesus in the Blessed Sacrament:
Sr Esther Mary

Obituary
11 Mar 1997 Sr Eudora, aged 95 years, professed 63 years

Community Publication
Associates' Newsletter, twice a year.

Community History
Valerie Bonham:
A Joyous Service: The Clewer Sisters and their Work
£7.95 + £1.25 p&p.
A Place in Life: The House of Mercy 1849-1883
£10.95 + £1.50 p&p.
The Sisters of the Raj: The Clewer Sisters in India
£12.95 + £2.00 p&p.

Guest and Retreat Facilities

CLEWER SPIRITUALITY CENTRE: the Community welcomes groups or individuals for retreats, conferences, quiet days, parish weekends, etc. Chapels, three spacious sitting rooms, two with libraries, two dining rooms, large garden, twenty-eight single rooms, four twin-bedded. All visitors are invited to share in the worship of the Community. Maximum for resident groups, thirty-six; non-resident, forty-five. Apply to the Administrator/Warden.

Oblates & Associates

CSJB has women oblates. Men and women may become associates or members of the Friends of Clewer.

A view of the grounds at Clewer, from the original House of Mercy, which is now part of the Spirituality Centre

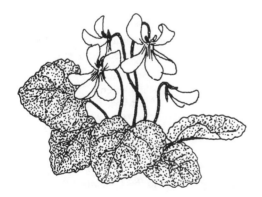

Has it ever struck you that every word spoken by Jesus is meant to liberate?

Donald Nicholl

Community of St John the Divine

CSJD

Founded 1848

*St John's House
652 Alum Rock Road
Birmingham
B8 3NS*

Tel: 0121 327 4174

Since the time of our foundation, we have always been a pioneering community. In the early years of our history, the Community played an important part in the establishing of new standards for Nursing and Midwifery, both in hospitals and in people's homes, as well as responding to health epidemics at home and abroad.

The Community has responded in more recent years to the challenge of change in Religious Life. The ethos of CSJD has broadened to cover all aspects of health, healing, reconciliation and pastoral care in its widest context ... ministries that all seek in helping people to find wholeness. The underpinning of our life and work is a spirituality based on St John, the Apostle of Love.

The exploration of the way ahead is based on much prayer, reflection and discussion. This is bringing to birth a new model for the Community. We now accept Lay members, who live with the Community for six months. This offers a structured life of prayer, work and study, which provides time and space for discernment of where God is leading each person. There is no expectation that Lay members will ask to enter the Noviciate, although this is one possibility, but it is broader in its aim. It is an encouragement for each member to explore their own spiritual journey and where the Lord is leading them.

We are still at the beginning of this new chapter. Yet as the Community celebrates its 150th Anniversary in 1998, we pray we may be open and responsive to God's leading and that there will be others called to share the challenge and commitment of our future direction.

The corporate life of the Community centres around a weekday daily Eucharist celebrated in the House and the fourfold Office taken from *Celebrating Common Prayer*. On Sundays, Sisters attend local churches of their choice.

MOTHER CHRISTINE
(Revd Mother Superior, assumed office Feb 1992)
SR MARGARET ANGELA *(Assistant Superior)*

Sr Audrey	Sr Jessica
Sr Margaret Faith	Sr Dorien
Sr Madeline	Sr Marie-Clare
Sr Teresa	Sr Pamela
Sr Monica	Sr Elaine

Novices: 2

Sr Ivy CR *(exploring transfer to this Community)*

Obituary
20 Sep 1997   Sr Susan, aged 80
years, professed 40 years

Community Publication
Annual Report

Community Wares
Various hand-crafted cards for different occasions.

Guest and Retreat Facilities
Quiet Days for individuals and groups.
Facilities for residential individual private retreats.

Associates
Associates are men and women from all walks of life who desire to have a close link with the Community. They are formally admitted and wear a distinctive cross of the Community. They make a simple commitment to God ... to the Community ... and to each other, and together with the Community they form a network of prayer, fellowship and mutual support within Christ's ministry of wholeness and reconciliation. Those eligible to be Associates are confirmed members of the Anglican Church or full members of other recognised Christian churches.

Friends of the Community
Friends of the Community are people who request their names to be put on our mailing list. They maintain a link with the Community and undertake to pray regularly for the Community.

Manage change carefully and boldly.
Be cautious when necessary.
Be bold when necessary.
Seek new forms
but do not reject the fundamental truths
you have received.
Donald Nicholl

Community of St Laurence

CSL

Founded 1874

*Convent of St Laurence
Field Lane
Belper
Derby
DE56 1DD*

*Tel: 01733 822585
& 823390*

The Community was founded by the Vicar of St Laurence's Church, Norwich, in 1874, with Ellen Lee as its first Mother. Its work was with the poor: not only the materially destitute, but also the poor in spirit, the poor in heart, the oppressed, widows and orphans, and all those who needed love and care. When Fr Hillyard moved to be Vicar of Christ Church, Belper, the sisters soon followed. They lived near the parish church until in 1882 the Convent was built.

For over a hundred years, the Community's work concentrated on caring for elderly women. In recent years, however, the work has mainly become retreats, conferences and teaching weekends. Some guests stay at the Convent for a few days peace and quiet, including over Christmas and Easter. One sister also works with the Omega Order at Winford Manor, near Bristol.

The Community has always been a small family, never at any time exceeding fourteen Sisters. Today, there are eight. The Community are willing to accept women in their forties and fifties, who are seeking a life of prayer in an active community and desire to give themselves to God to test their vocation in Religious Life.

MOTHER JEAN MARY CSL
(Mother Superior, assumed office 1995)
8 professed Sisters

Community Publication
Gridiron, which is free of charge.

Associates
Associates pray regularly for the community, and include priests and lay people. There are days organised at the Convent for the associates, at which new members may be admitted, and also retreats.

Community Wares
Crafts.

Guest and Retreat Facilities
Twenty-four single and seven twin rooms.

Chapel and Convent of Saint Laurence, Belper

Community of St Mary the Virgin

CSMV

Founded 1848

St Mary's Convent
Challow Road
Wantage
Oxfordshire
OX12 9DJ

Tel: 01235 763141

The Community of St Mary the Virgin was founded in 1848 by William John Butler, then Vicar of Wantage, and this year, it celebrates its 150th Anniversary. As Sisters, we are called to respond to our vocation in the spirit of the Blessed Virgin Mary: "Behold, I am the handmaid of the Lord. Let it be to me according to your word." Our common life is centred in the worship of God through the Eucharist, the daily Office and in personal prayer. From this all else flows. For some it will be expressed in outgoing ministry in neighbourhood and parish, or in living alongside those in inner city areas. For others, it will be expressed in spiritual direction, preaching and retreat giving, in creative work in studio and press, or in forms of healing ministry. Sisters also live and work among the elderly at St Katharine's House, our dual-registered Home for Elderly People in Wantage. The Community has been in India and South Africa for many years and has involvement in the nurturing and training of a small indigenous community in Madagascar.

MOTHER BARBARA CLAIRE
(Reverend Mother, assumed office 8 Dec 1997)

The Community numbers ninety-nine Sisters and has a Noviciate which normally numbers about six.

Obituaries
Sr Barbara Bernardine, Sr Gertrude Constance, Sr Jane Monica & Sr Verity all died in 1997.

Community History
A Hundred Years of Blessing, SPCK, London, 1946

Community Wares
The Printing Press offers a variety of cards. Catalogues are available from the Sister in charge of the Press at St Mary's Convent.

Guest and Retreat Facilities
ST MARY'S CONVENT   The Sisters welcome to the Guest Wing those who wish to spend time in rest, retreat and silence within the setting of a Religious Community. Our particular emphasis is on hospitality to individuals, and where requested we try to arrange individual guidance with a Sister. We are also able to accommodate a small number of groups for retreats and Quiet Days.

ST PETER'S BOURNE   This is a retreat house especially suitable for individual guests or small groups. Resident guests have the use of a large sitting room overlooking the garden, as well as Chapel and library. Day groups are accommodated separately in the 'Coachhouse' where the facilities are self-catering. All guests are welcome to join in the daily Eucharist.

Oblates

The Oblates of the Community respond to their vocation in the same spirit as Mary: "Behold, I am the handmaid of the Lord. Let it be to me according to your word." Their vocation runs in parallel to that of the Sisters but is distinct. Oblates may be married or single, women or men, ordained or lay. The majority are Anglicans, but members of other denominations are also accepted. Each is linked with the Community through visits to the Convent or other Community houses, and by regular contact with the Oblate Sister. Each is also linked with the whole Oblate body by the bond of a shared commitment, and they support each other in prayer and fellowship. There is a common Rule, based on Scripture and the Rule of St Augustine, and each Oblate also draws up a personal Rule of Life in consultation with the Oblate Sister. The distinguishing mark of the Oblate commitment is that they promise to share in the saying of the Divine Office (at least one Office a day). The process of discernment is quite searching. An Enquirer may spend as much as a year exploring the possibility of an Oblate vocation. After admission as a Novice Oblate, there is a period of at least two years, during which the vocation is tested, and quarterly reports made to the Oblate Sister. Only then may a Novice Oblate ask to go forward to full Oblation. The promises made then are renewed annually. There are at present 105 Oblates in the UK, twelve Novice Oblates and fourteen Enquirers.

Associates

Our Associates are men and women, ordained and lay, Anglican and other denominations, who, after coming into contact with the Community, wish to be linked in a closer way with our life and prayer. As well as praying daily for the Community, Associates are asked to draw up their own Rule of Life, based on certain guidelines: these include daily prayer and Bible-reading, regular attendance at the Eucharist and an annual retreat. Each year three retreats of three to four days are held at the Convent for Associates.

There is no set probationary period, but when an Associate-enquirer and the Associates' Sister both feel it is right, a date is fixed for Admission, and this usually takes place in the Convent. Every Associate receives a monthly letter on some aspect of the Community's life and work, and also a quarterly intercession leaflet. In addition, an Associates' Day is held annually at the Convent and Associates are encouraged at other times to link up with those who live in their area or to attend informal meetings arranged by the Associates' Sister.

At present, there are some 230 Associates in the UK as well as many others in countries where the Community has had or still has Community houses. There are always a number of Associate enquirers, normally about fifteen at any given time.

Tel: 0181 445 5535
4 Hilton Road
Leeds
LS8 4HB
Tel: 0113 262 7681

St Peter's Bourne
40 Oakleigh Park South
London
N20 9JN

366 High Street
Smethwick
West Midlands
B66 3PD
Tel: 0121 558 0094

St Katharine's House
Ormond Road
Wantage
Oxfordshire
OX12 9DH
Tel: 01235 762739

St Mary's Lodge
Challow Road
Wantage
Oxfordshire
OX12 9DH
Tel: 01235 767112

Christa Prema Seva Sangha
Shivajinagar
Pune 4115005
Maharastra
INDIA

3 Keurboom Avenue
Omega Park
Brakpan 1541
SOUTH AFRICA

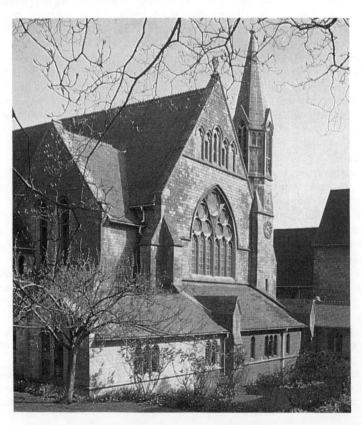

St Mary's Convent, Wantage

Community of St Peter

CSP

Founded 1861

St Peter's Convent
Maybury Hill
Woking
Surrey
GU22 8AE

Tel: 01483 761137

St Columba's House
(Retreat &Conference
Centre)
Maybury Hill
Woking
Surrey
GU22 8AE

Tel: 01483 766498

The Sisters have registered homes (nursing/care) for elderly women and women workers in need of a protected environment. St Columba's Retreat House is under their care and they also have close links with the Society of the Holy Cross (a sisterhood founded by St Peter's Community in Korea, see overseas section).

The Daily Office and Eucharist are arranged at St Columba's according to the wishes of groups attending, with the sisters working in the House sharing their worship, or saying the Office privately or returning to the Convent.

REVD MOTHER MARGARET PAUL
(Mother Superior, assumed office 1973)
SR ROSAMUND *(Assistant Superior)*

Sr Hilary	Sr Angela
Sr Dorothy	Sr Teresa Mary
Sr Constance Margaret	Sr Joyce
Sr Margery Grace	Sr Georgina Ruth
Sr Joy	Sr Lucy Clare
Sr Jane Margery	*Novices : 1*

Obituaries
5 Jan 1997   Sr Rachel Mary Buswell, aged 82 years
15 Jan 1997   Sr Catherine Joan Glover, aged 86 years

Community Publication
Associates' leaflet at Christmas and Pentecost.

Community History
Elizabeth Cuthbert, *In St Peter's Shadow*, CSP, Woking, 1994.

Guest and Retreat Facilities
ST COLUMBA'S HOUSE, recently refurbished, has a purpose-built retreat and conference centre. It can accommodate twenty-four. Enquiries should be addressed to the Director.

Community Wares
Cards.

Associates
The associates' fellowship meets twice a year at Pentecost and Christmas. The associates support the community in prayer and with practical help, as they are able. They have a simple rule, sharing a daily Office and attending the Eucharist as their individual commitments permit.

Community of St Peter, Horbury

CSPH

Founded 1858

St Peter's Convent
Dovecote Lane
Horbury
Wakefield
West Yorkshire
WF4 6BB

Tel: 01924 272181

The Community seeks to glorify God by a life of loving dedication to him, by worship and by serving him in others. A variety of pastoral work is undertaken including retreat and mission work, social work and ministry to individuals in need. The spirit of the community is Benedictine and the recitation of the Divine Office central to the life.

MOTHER ROBINA
(Mother Superior, assumed office 14 Apr 1993)
SR ELIZABETH *(Assistant Superior)*

Sr Veronica
Sr Gwynneth Mary
Sr Margaret
Sr Mary Clare *(priest)*
Sr Phyllis
Sr Jean Clare
Sr Monica

Sr Margaret Ann, 2 Main St., Bossall, York YO2 7NT
Tel: 01904 468253

Community Publication
Annual Report

Guest and Retreat Facilities
A separate guest wing has four single rooms, with shower room and utility room.

Oblates and Associates
The Community has both oblates and associates.

Lauds
6.30 am

Mass
7.30 am

Midday Office
12.00 noon

Vespers
6.00 pm

Compline
9.00 pm

Community of the Servants of the Cross

CSC

Founded 1877

*Marriott House
Tollhouse Close
Chichester
PO19 3EZ*

Tel: 01243 781620

The Community has an Augustinian Rule and for much of their history the sisters have cared for elderly and infirm women. In 1997, the Sisters left their convent at Lindfield in Sussex and some moved to Marriott House, a retirement home in Chichester, and others to the Community of St Peter at Woking. They are now known as:

MOTHER ANGELA AND THE HOLY ROOD SISTERS.

They use a local church for Mass and the Offices.

MOTHER ANGELA (*Mother Superior*)

9 Professed sisters

Dürer's 'Calvary' (circa 1502)

Community of the Servants of the Will of God

CSWG

Founded 1953

*The Monastery of the
Holy Trinity
Crawley Down
Crawley
West Sussex
RH10 4LH*

Tel: 01342 712074

*Vigils
5.00 am*

*Lauds
7.00 am*

*Terce
9.30 am*

*Sext
12.00 noon*

*None
1.45 pm*

*Vespers
6.30 pm*

*Mass
7.00 pm Mon - Fri
11.00 am Sat & Sun*

This monastery is set in woodland with a small farm attached. The Community lives a contemplative life, uniting silence, work and prayer in a simple life style based on the Rule of St Benedict. The Community is especially concerned with uniting the traditions of East and West, and has developed the Liturgy, Divine Office and use of the Jesus Prayer accordingly. The Community has another monastery at Hove, living under the same Rule, so as to bring Christ into this Urban Priority Area through the life of prayer. Both monasteries now include women living under the same monastic Rule.

FATHER GREGORY
(Father Superior, assumed office 14 Sep 1973)
FATHER BRIAN *(Senior Monk)*

CRAWLEY DOWN	HOVE
Fr Gregory *(Superior)*	Fr Brian *(Prior)*
Fr Colin *(Prior)*	Br Mark
Fr Peter	Br Martin
Br Christopher Mark	Sr Mary Angela
Br John Baptist	Br Steven
Br John of the Cross	Sr Mary Esther
Br Andrew	Br Seraphim
Sr Mary Ruth	
Novices: 2	

The Monastery of Christ the Saviour
23 Cambridge Rd, Hove, East Sussex BN3 1DE
Tel: 01273 726698

Community Publication
CSWG *Newsletter*, issued Advent & Pentecost. Write to the Monastery of the Holy Trinity.

Guest and Retreat Facilities
CRAWLEY DOWN: six individual guest rooms; meals in community refectory; Divine Office and Eucharist, all with modal chant.

HOVE: two individual guest rooms; other facilities comparable to Crawley Down.

Community Wares
Mounted icon prints, Jesus Prayer ropes, booklets on monastic and spiritual life.

Associates
The associates keep a rule of life in the spirit of the monasteries.

Chapel of Our Lady & the Holy Angels

and Hermitages,
Community of the Servants of the Will of God, Crawley Down

Community of the Sisters of the Church

CSC

Founded 1870

Founded by Emily Ayckbowm in 1870, the Community of the Sisters of the Church is an international body of women within the Anglican Communion, living under the gospel values of Poverty, Chastity and Obedience, desiring to be faithful to the traditions of Religious Life while exploring new ways of expressing them and of living community life and ministry today. By our worship, ministry and life in community, we desire to be channels of the reconciling love and acceptance of Christ, to acknowledge the dignity of every person, and to enable others to encounter the living God whom we seek.

The houses have varying timetables of corporate worship. The Eucharist and Divine Office (usually fourfold) are the heart of our Community life.

SR ANITA
(Mother Superior, assumed office Feb 1998)

Aileen	Gillian	Mary Adela
Annaliese	Heather	Mary Josephine
Annie	Helen	Mercy
Ann Mechtilde	Hilda Mary	Miriam
Audrey	Jennifer	Muriel
Benedetta	Jennifer Betty	Phyllis
Bernadette	Joanna	Rebecca
Beryl	Joy	Rita
Catherine	Judith	Robin Elizabeth
Carolyn	Kathleen	Rosina
Carrie	Kim Marie	Ruth
Christina	Lilian	Ruth Anne
Doreen	Linda Mary	Sarah
Dorothea	Lydia	Scholastica
Elizabeth May	Lynn	Sheila Julian
Elisa Helen	Marietta	Susan
Ellen	Marina	Valerie
Elsa	Margaret	Vivien
Elspeth	Marguerite	
Fiona	Marguerite Mae	*Novices:* 15
Frances	Martha	*Postulants:* 7

Obituaries

8 Apr 1997   Sr Lila (Smith), aged 84 years, professed 53 years

16 Feb 1998   Sr Philomena (Bell), aged 81 years, professed 54 years

Houses in England

St Michael's Convent	St Gabriel's	10 Furness Road
56 Ham Common	27A Dial Road	West Harrow
Richmond	Clevedon	Middlesex
Surrey TW10 7JH	Avon BS21 7HL	HA2 0RL
Tel: 0181 940 8711	*Tel: 01275 872586*	*Tel & Fax: 0181 423 3780*
& 0181 948 2502		
Fax: 0181 332 2927	82 Ashley Road	
	Bristol	
112 St Andrew's Rd Nth	BS6 5NT	
Lytham St Annes	*Tel: 01179 413268*	
Lancashire FY8 2JQ	*Fax: 01179 086620*	
Tel: 01253 728016		

Houses in Canada

St Michael's House	19 Cardinal Mindszenty Boulevard
127 Burgundy Road	St Elizabeth Village
Oakville	Hamilton
Ontario L6J 6R1	Ontario L9B 2M3
Tel: +1 905 844 9511	*Tel & Fax: +1 905 387 5659*
Fax:+1 905 842 6529	

Houses in Australia

216 Mahoney's Road	The House of Prayer	96 Hertford Street
East Burwood	42 Wirrang Drive	Glebe
Victoria 3151	Dondingalong	NSW 2037
Tel: +613 9802 1955	Via Kempsey	*Tel: +612 660 5708*
Fax: +613 9802 6642	NSW 2440	*Fax: +612 9692 0173*
	Tel: +612 65 669 244	
44/1 St Kilda Road	*Fax: +616 566 9165*	
St Kilda		
Victoria 3182		
Tel & Fax: +613 9593 9590		

*In a controversy,
enter it knowing that you will ask the other
to bless you at the end.
Skill is needed for that
and a clean heart.*

Donald Nicholl

Houses in the Solomon Islands

PO Box A7	Patteson House	Tetete ni Kolivuti
Auki	Box 510	Box 510
Malaita	Honiara	Honiara
	Tel: +677 22413	
	Fax: +677 21098	

St Gabriel's
c/o Hanuato'o Diocese
Kira Kira
Makira/Ulawa Province
Tel: +677 50128

St Mary's
Luesala
Diocese of Temotu
Santa Cruz

Affiliated Communities

Society of Our Lady St Mary
Bethany Place
PO Box 762
Digby
Nova Scotia BOV 1AO
CANADA

Community of the Love of God
Nazareth
Kadampanad South 691553
Pathanamthitta District
Kerala
INDIA

Community Publication

Newsletter, three times a year, the editor of which is Sr Audrey in Australia (St Kilda address). However, information can be obtained from any house of the community.

Community Wares

These vary from house to house, but some sell crafts and cards. Vestments are made in the Solomon Islands.

Guest and Retreat Facilities

Hospitality is offered in most houses. Where it is the main ministry, the accommodation, facilities and programmes are appointed and shaped to this end. Facilities vary from house to house and so contact should be made with a particular house for specific details.

Associates

Associates are men and women who seek to live the Gospel values of Simplicity, Chastity and Obedience within their own circumstances. Each creates his/her own Rule of Life and has a Link Sister or Link House. They are united in spirit with CSC in its life of worship and service, fostering a mutually enriching bond.

Community of the Sisters of the Love of God

SLG

A contemplative community whose chief work is prayer built on the offering of the Eucharist (daily at the Mother House) and the regular recitation of the Divine Office by day and night. Life and prayer in solitude is recognised as an important part of the Sisters' vocation, in accordance with the Carmelite spirit of the community.

MOTHER ROSEMARY
(Reverend Mother, assumed office 1996)

Sisters in profession: 45
Novices: 5 *Postulants:* 1

Founded 1906

*Convent
of the Incarnation
Fairacres
Oxford
OX4 1TB*

Tel: 01865 721301

*Bede House
Pinnock Lane
Staplehurst
Tonbridge, Kent
TN12 0HQ*

Tel: 01580 891262

*Convent of St Mary &
the Angels
Woodland Avenue
Hemel Hempstead
Hertfordshire
HP1 1RG*

Tel: 01442 256989

Obituaries

18 Apr 1997	Sr Hilda Mary, aged 93 years, professed 61 years
1 Aug 1997	Sr Irene Mary, aged 88 years, professed 38 years

St Isaac's Retreat, PO Box 93, Opononi, Northland, Aoteoroa/New Zealand

Community Publication
Fairacres Chronicle Write to the Sister in charge, SLG Press, Convent of the Incarnation, Fairacres, Oxford OX4 1TB.

Community Wares
SLG Press publishes books and pamphlets on spirituality. A list of titles is available from the above address.

Guest and Retreat Facilities
There is limited accommodation for private retreats, for both men and women, at all houses of the Community. Please write to the Sister in Charge to make a booking.

Oblates and associates
The Community includes Oblate Sisters, who are called to the contemplative life in the world rather than within the monastic enclosure. There are several other groups of associates: Priest Associates, Companions, and the Fellowship of the Love of God. Information about all these may be obtained from the Reverend Mother at Fairacres.

Ewell Monastery

Founded 1966

Ewell Monastery
Water Lane
West Malling
Kent
ME19 6HH

A Cistercian Community. The monks live the contemplative life according to the Rule of St Benedict in prayer, reading, and work within the monastery.

Fr Aelred Arnesen *(Abba)*

Br Timothy Pritchard

Guest and Retreat Facilities
There is a small guest house for visitors. Please write to make a reservation, giving alternative dates.

Associates
Friends of Ewell Monastery.

> *I am glad of monasteries and hermitages,*
> *however critical I sometimes feel.*
> *Oases of sanity and peace to remind the world,*
> *which is full of noise, words, money, power and sex,*
> *that all these things can never satisfy the longings*
> *of the human heart.*
> *Donald Nicholl*

Oratory of the Good Shepherd

OGS

Founded 1913

The Oratory of the Good Shepherd is a society of priests and laymen founded at Cambridge, which now has provinces in North America, Australia, Southern Africa and Great Britain.

Oratorians are bound together by a common Rule and discipline; members do not generally live together in community but foster the common life through prayer, and regular meetings in chapter and retreat.

At the heart of the Oratorian's life are the seven 'Notes' which provide the ideal for his life as an individual and with his brethren, and the daily spiritual rule is designed to help him carry out his vocation of worship and service in communion with Jesus the Good Shepherd. Consecration of life in the Oratory has the twin purpose of fostering the individual brother's personal search for God in union with his brethren, and as a sign of the Kingdom. So through the apostolic work of the brethren, the Oratory seeks to make a contribution to the life and witness of the whole Church.

In common with traditional communities, the Oratory requires celibacy. However, brothers are not required to surrender capital, though they are accountable to their brethren for their spending and are expected to live simply and with generosity. The ideal spiritual pattern includes daily Eucharist, Offices and an hour of prayer. 'Labour of the mind' is a characteristic of the life and members are expected to spend some time in study. The brethren are grouped in 'colleges' and meet regularly for prayer and support, and each province meets annually for retreat and chapter. Every three years, the General Chapter meets, presided over by the Superior of the whole Oratory, whose responsibility is to maintain the unity of the provinces.

Those who want to test their vocation as Oratorians have a period of postulancy, before being admitted to probation (or noviciate) which may last one or two years. During this time, the new brother is cared for and nurtured in the Oratory life by another brother of his College. The brother may then, with the consent of the province, make his first profession, which is renewed annually for at least five years, though with the hope of intention and perseverance for life. After five years, profession can be made for a longer period, and after ten years a brother may, with the consent of the whole Oratory, make his profession for life.

THE VERY REVEREND JOHN SALT OGS *(Superior)*
The Deanery, PO Box 207, Eshowe 2815, Zululand, South Africa

Brethren world-wide: 49 professed, 3 probationers

The Community in the UK
THE RT REVD LINDSAY URWIN OGS
(UK Provincial, assumed office 1996)
Bishop's House, 21 Guildford Rd, Horsham, RH12 1LU
Tel: 01403 211139; Fax: 01403 217349; E-Mail: bishhorsham@clara.net

George Briggs	Malcolm King
Brian Oman	Michael Carmichael
Robert Symonds	Geoffrey Bostock
George Braund	James Finnemore
John Thorold	Brian Lee
Thomas Gresley-Summers	Michael Bullock
David Jowitt	Christopher Powell
Michael Bootes	Peter Walker
Peter Ford	Michael Longstaffe
Michael Bartlett	Nicholas Gandy
David Johnson	Charles Macrae
Dominic Walker	
Clive McCleester	*Probationers:* 1

Companions and Associates
The Oratory has an extended family of Companions, with their own rule of life, and Associates. Companionship is open to men and women, lay or ordained, married or single.

Community History
George Tibbatts, *The Oratory of the Good Shepherd: The First Seventy-five Years*, The Almoner OGS, Windsor, 1988.

Order of the Holy Paraclete

OHP

Founded 1915

St Hilda's Priory
Sneaton Castle
Whitby
N Yorks
YO21 3QN

Tel: 01947 602079
Fax: 01947 820854

Morning Prayer
7.15 am
(7.25 am Sat,
7.45 am Sun)

Midday Office
12.15 pm

Mass
12.30 pm
(8.00 am Sat,
8.30 am & 10.30 am Sun)

Vespers
5.30 pm (4.30 pm Fri)

Compline
9.00 pm
(informal on Fri)

Times are subject to
alteration: please check
in advance.

Although founded as an educational Order, the Sisters have now diversified their work to include hospitality, development work overseas, inner city involvement, retreats and spiritual direction. The main house of the Order is St Hilda's Priory, Whitby. There are houses in Ghana, South Africa and Swaziland as well as in Leicester, York, Rievaulx and Boston Spa (Martin House Children's Hospice). Central to the Order's life are the Divine Office and Eucharist, a strong emphasis on corporate activity, and a lively interest in the Celtic Church and the early saints of Northern Britain.

SR JANET
(Prioress, elected 14 Feb 1994)
SR JANET ELIZABETH *(Sub Prioress)*

Sr Mary Frances	Sr Alicia
Sr Bridget Mary	Sr Michelle
Sr Kathleen	Sr Truda
Sr Mary Dorothea	Sr Mary Nina
Sr Barbara	Sr Stella Mary
Sr Beatrice	Sr Lucy
Sr Eileen	Sr Naomi
Sr Mary	Sr Heather
Sr Rachel	Sr Muriel
Sr Jean	Sr Mary Margaret
Sr Ursula	Sr Anita
Sr Barbara Maude	Sr Margaret Shirley
Sr Sophia	Sr Hilary
Sr Margaret Irene	Sr Nancye
Sr Bertha	Sr Birgit
Sr Olive	Sr Patricia
Sr Francis Clare	Sr Gillian
Sr Marjorie	Sr Hilary Joy
Sr Rosa	Sr Maureen
Sr Rosalind	Sr Grace
Sr Constance	Sr Janette
Sr Catherine	Sr Betty
Sr Sheila	Sr Marion
Sr Philippa	Sr Dorothy Stella
Sr Alison	Sr Benedicta

Sr Caroline	Sr Margaret Anne	Sr Rachel Clare
Sr Margaret Elizabeth	Sr Susan	Sr Linda
Sr Marion Eva	Sr Jocelyn	Sr Aba
Sr Judith	Sr Barbara Ann	Sr Pam
Sr Heather Francis	Sr Carole	Sr Helen
Sr Erika	Sr Mavis	*Novices:* 1
Sr Maureen Ruth	Sr Kate	

Obituaries

24 Jun 1997   Sr Jane, aged 50 years, professed 23 years
25 Jul 1997   Sr Miriam, aged 89 years, professed 50 years

Martin House
Grove Road
Clifford
Wetherby LS23 6TX
Tel: 01937 843449

The Abbey Cottage
Rievaulx
York YO6 5LB
Tel: 01439 798209

Beach Cliff
14 North Promenade
Whitby
N Yorks YO21 3JX
Tel: 01947 601968

St Oswald's Pastoral Centre
Woodlands Drive
Sleights, Whitby
N Yorks YO21 1RY
Tel: 01947 810496

21 Honeygreen Road
Flat 5
Dundee DD4 8BD
Tel: 01382-509206

St Michael's House
15 Portman Street
Belgrave
Leicester LE24 6NZ
Tel: 0116 266 7805

7 Minster Yard
York YO1 2JD
Tel: 01904 620601

PO Box 594
Accra
GHANA
Tel: + 233 21 556675

St Benedict's Retreat
House
PO Box 27
Rosettenville 2130
SOUTH AFRICA
Tel & Fax: + 27 11 435 3662

St Hilda's House,
PO Box 1272
Manzini
SWAZILAND
Tel: + 268 53323
Fax: + 268 54083

PO Box 3811
Manzini
SWAZILAND
Tel & Fax: +268 57222

Community Publication
OHP Newsletter, twice a year. Write to The Publications Secretary at St Hilda's Priory.

Community History
A Foundation Member, *Fulfilled in Joy*, Hodder & Stoughton, 1964.

Community Wares
Cards and crafts.

Guest and Retreat Facilities
St Hilda's Priory: nine rooms (six single; two double; one twin) in the Priory or nearby houses. Individuals or small groups are welcome for personal quiet or retreat, day or residential. If asked in advance, some guidance can be provided.

There is no programme of retreats at the Priory. Larger groups are invited to contact the Manager of Sneaton Castle Centre (at the Priory address), where facilities are available for up to a hundred guests.

St Oswald's Pastoral Centre: eight single rooms, four twin-bedded rooms. The Centre can take up to twelve people singly or sixteen when sharing. There is also The Grimston Room which can hold up to forty people for Quiet Days or Conferences. There is a chapel, two lounges, a small but useful library, and a kitchen where guests can make hot drinks or snacks. All bedrooms have hot and cold water and are heated. The cost of maintaining the Centre is met from the donations of guests. Bookings and enquiries can be made to the Sister-in-charge, enclosing a stamped addressed envelope.

Tertiaries and Associates

The OHP Tertiary Order is a fellowship of women and men, united under a common discipline, based on the OHP Rule, and supporting one another in their discipleship. Tertiaries are ordinary Christians seeking to offer their lives in the service of Christ, helping the Church and showing love in action. They value their links with each other and with the Sisters of the Order, at Whitby and elsewhere, and when possible they meet together for mutual support in prayer, discussion and ministry. The Tertiary Order is open to communicant members of any Trinitarian Church.

The OHP Associates are friends of the Order who desire to keep in touch with its life and work while serving God in their various spheres. Many have made initial contact with the Sisters through a visit or parish mission, or via another Associate. All are welcome, married or single, clergy or lay, regardless of religious affiliation.

The Priory and Chapel, Sneaton Castle, Order of the Holy Paraclete

Order of St Benedict

Alton Abbey

OSB

Founded 1884

Alton Abbey
Abbey Road
Beech, Alton
Hampshire
GU34 4AP

Tel: 01420 562145
& 563575
Fax: 01420 561691

The Community, now dedicated to Our Lady and Saint John, was founded on the work undertaken among sailors in Burma and India from 1884 by the Reverend Charles Plomer Hopkins. From 1896, the Community concentrated its activities at the mother house at Alton (1895 to the present), with priories at Barry (1894 - 1912) and Greenwich (1899 - 1951). The active work among seamen was discontinued in 1989; the Community continues to administer the Seamen's Friendly Society as a charitable trust. Having observed the Rule of St Benedict from 1893, the Community formally adopted the Rule on 28 January 1981, when new constitutions received ratification from the Visitor.

RT REVD DOM GILES HILL
(Abbot, elected 12 Sep 1990)
VERY REVD DOM WILLIAM HUGHES *(Prior)*

Revd Dom Peter Roundhill
Dom Andrew Johnson
Revd Dom Nicholas Seymour *(Novice Master)*
Dom Stephen Hoare
Dom Anselm Shobrook
Rt Revd Timothy Bavin

Community Publication
The Messenger, occasional, write to the Abbey.

The Vigil
5.30 am

Morning Prayer
7.15 am

Mass
9.00 am
(10 am Sun & Solemnities)

Midday Prayer
12.00 noon

Evening Prayer
5.00 pm

Night Prayer
8.30 pm   (7.30 pm Sun)

Guest and Retreat Facilities
Guest house facilities for up to eighteen persons, for both group and individual retreats. There is a programme of retreats each year, which is available from the Guestmaster.

Community Wares
Altar bread department: contact Dom Stephen Hoare.

Oblates
For details of the Oblates of St Benedict, please contact the Oblate Master.

Order of
St Benedict

Burford
Priory

OSB

Founded 1941

Priory of Our Lady
Priory Lane, Burford
Oxfordshire
OX18 4SQ

Tel: 01993 823605

Lauds
6.45 am
(7.00 am Sun &
Solemnities)

Terce
9.00 am

Mass
12.00 noon (10.30 am Sun)

None
2.00 pm

Vespers
5.30 pm

Compline
9.00 pm
(8.30 pm, Sat &
Eve of Solemnities Vigil)

The Priory is home to a mixed Community of nuns and monks who live a shared life under the Rule of St Benedict, observing the traditional balance between prayer, study and manual work. Members of the Community do not normally undertake outside engagements, but help to support themselves by their ministry of hospitality at the Community's small retreat and guest house and by various works undertaken within the enclosure. They are largely responsible themselves for the upkeep of the Priory, its extensive garden, grounds and woodland.

VERY REVD BROTHER STUART BURNS
(Prior, elected 14 Oct 1996)
Sister Scholastica Newman
Sister Mary Bernard Taylor
Brother Thomas Quin *(Novice Guardian)*
Brother Anthony Hare

Novices: 1
Postulants: 4

Obituary
23 Sep 1997   Sister Joseph Bocock, aged 91 years, professed 52 years, Prioress 1979-84

Guest and Retreat Facilities
Eight-bedroomed retreat house, with four single rooms and four twin-bedded rooms.

Community Wares
Block mounted icon prints.
Mounted photograph cards.
Printing (hand press) cards and letter heads.

Oblates and Friends
There is a small group of Oblates and a Friends' Association.

Order of St Benedict

Community of St Mary at the Cross, Edgware

OSB

Founded 1866

St Mary at the Cross
Priory Field Drive
Hale Lane, Edgware
Middlesex
HA8 9PZ

Tel: 0181 958 7868
Fax: 0181 958 1920

Readings and Lauds
7.00 am (7.30 am Sun)

Midday Office
11.55 am (except Sun)

Vespers
5.30 pm (4.40 pm Fri)

Monastic Night Prayer
7.30 pm

Mass
7.45 am Weekdays
11.00 am once a week
10.30 am Sun & special
feasts

The Community has cared for disabled people throughout its history. This work, now including the care of frail elderly people, continues today in Henry Nihill House, a modern residential/nursing home under the Director of Care. The Community gives priority to prayer and worship in the Divine Office and Eucharist and its ministry of intercession. A growing number of people and parishes are united in the Community's prayer through its 'Prayer Link'.

RT REVD DAME MARY THÉRÈSE ZELENT
(Abbess, elected 30 March 1993)
VERY REVD DAME BARBARA JOHNSON *(Prioress)*

Dame Rosemary Francis Breeze
Dame Raphael Mary Pay
(Former Superior, Servants of Christ)
Dame Dorothea Haviland
Dame Teresa Mary Hastie
Dame Jane Frances Franklin

Intern Oblate: 1

Ethiopian Orthodox:
Sr Atsedc Bekele
Sr Tirsit Eguale

Community Publication
Abbey Newsletter, yearly. Write to St Mary's Convent.

Community Wares
Cards.

Guest and Retreat Facilities
Easily accessible from the M1, the Convent offers an excellent day Conference Centre, and guest accommodation for rest or retreat, and space for Quiet days. The monastic experience can be shared by people wishing to take 'time out' for up to three months.

Guest accommodation
LORETO – a small, comfortable guest house with seven bedrooms. Hospitality for up to two weeks for rest and retreat.
HERMITAGE – a one-bedroom flatlet, self-contained but not self-catering, which is ideal for a time of real quiet.
QUIET DAYS – For those needing space in their lives and a

day of reflection, prayer or study, we can provide a room and make you feel at home.

Special arrangements can be made with Mother Abbess for those who cannot afford to pay the recommended tariff.

Day Conference Centre
Open 9 am to 6 pm (Closed Holy Week and Christmas Week).

The centre has space for about fifty people. It is ideal for church and social groups, training days, family parties, etc.

Requests for booking forms may be made by post or telephone, Monday to Friday. There is a non-returnable £10 deposit with each booking.

Convent & Refectory of the Community of St Mary at the Cross, Edgware

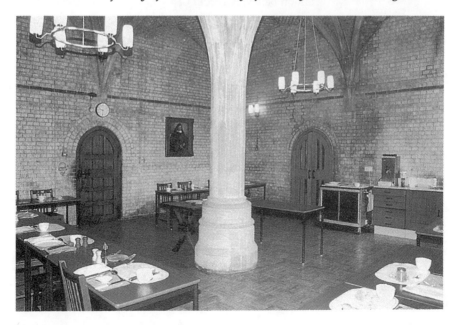

Order of St Benedict

Elmore Abbey

OSB

Founded 1914

Elmore Abbey
Church Lane
Speen, Newbury
Berkshire
RG14 1SA

Tel: 01635 33080

Vigils
5.30 am

Lauds
8.00 am

Terce
10.00 am

Sext
12.00 noon

None
4.00 pm

Vespers
6.00 pm

Compline
8.30 pm

Mass:
8.00 am Mon - Sat
(with Lauds)
10.30 am Sun (Parish
Church)

The monastery aims to provide an environment within which the traditional monastic balance between worship, study and work may be maintained with a characteristic Benedictine stress upon corporate worship and community life. To this end, outside commitments are kept to a minimum.

RT REVD DOM BASIL MATTHEWS
(Abbot, elected 3 Jul 1988)
VERY REVD DOM FRANCIS HUTCHISON *(Prior)*

Revd Dom Boniface Nielsen   Dom Bruce De Walt
Dom Mark Alberic Brierly   Br Hugh Kelly
Rt Revd Dom Kenneth   Fr Peter Aelred Packer
  Newing *(Novice Master)*   *Novices: 2*
Dom Simon Jarrett   *Postulants: 1*

Obituaries

20 Jan 1997	Revd Dom Augustine Morris, aged 91, professed 72 years
19 Jul 1997	Revd Dom Godfrey Stokes, aged 93, professed 52 years

Community Publication
Elmore Abbey Record, yearly, write to the Cellarer.
Books:
Augustine Morris, *Oblates: Life with Saint Benedict* £4.25.
Simon Bailey, *A Tactful God: Gregory Dix*, £12.99.

Community Wares
Incense: 500g packets made at the Abbey.
Brands: Glastonbury £8; Rievaulx £7.25; Evesham £7.50; Sherborne £7; Charcoal: Swift light, 80 small rings £5.25.
Contact: The Cellarer, Elmore Abbey.

Guest and Retreat Facilities
There is a small guest house with accommodation for up to four wishing to stay for a personal retreat or period of quiet. Guests are admitted to the Oratory, the Guests' Common Room, the Refectory and the front garden.

Oblates
An extended confraternity of oblates, numbering over 350 men and women, married and single, seek to live according to a rule of life inspired by Benedictine principles. From the start, the community has believed in the importance of prayer for Christian unity and the fostering of ecumenism. Details can be obtained from the Oblate Master.

Order of
St Benedict

Malling
Abbey

OSB

Founded 1891

St Mary's Abbey
52 Swan Street
West Malling, Kent
ME19 6JX

Tel: 01732 843309

S aint Benedict sees the monastery as a school of the Lord's service where a united community endeavours to grow in stability, conversion of life and obedience within the enclosure. The call of God is the essential requirement for admission to the noviciate to share in the life of prayer, study and manual work in the house and grounds. The period of training before final profession is normally five and a half years. The guest house offers hospitality to those wishing to share the worship and peace of Saint Mary's Abbey for a few days.

MOTHER ABBESS MARY JOHN MARSHALL
(elected 27 Sep 1990)
SR MARY PAUL COLLINS *(Prioress)*

M Perpetua Towell	Sr Mary Gundulf Wood
Sr Mary Augustine Dalgarno	Sr Mary David Best
Sr Macrina Banner	Sr Anna Bowes
Sr Martina Michael	Sr Mary Stephen Packwood
Sr Anastasia Feast	Sr Felicity Spencer
Sr Mary Gregory Barrett	Sr Gabriel Allatt
Sr Mary Mark Brooksbank	Sr Bartimaeus Ives
Sr Mary Ignatius Conklin	Sr Raphael Stone
Sr Mary Simon Corbett	Sr Seonaid Crabtree
Sr Ruth Blackmore	Sr Alison Buttolph
Sr Mary Cuthbert Archer	Sr Mary Magdalen Long
Sr Mary Francis Tillard	*Junior professed*: 4
Sr Mary Anselm Topley	*Novices:* 1

Obituaries

3 Jun 1997   Sr Elizabeth Roger-Smith, aged 93 years, professed 56 years

31 Oct 1997   Sr Clare King, aged 87 years, professed 38 years

Community Wares
There are cards and booklets printed and painted at the abbey on sale at the Guest House.

Guest and Retreat Facilities
We offer no organised retreats apart from those for our oblates. Those wishing to make a private retreat are welcome to do so at the Guest House.

Oblates
Oblates are men and women who feel called by God to follow the Benedictine way, but outside the cloister. They affirm their baptismal commitment by a promise of con-

Vigils
4.30 am   (5.00 am Sun)

Lauds
6.50 am   (8.10 am Sun)

Eucharist
7.30 am   (9.00 am Sun)

Terce
8.35 am

Sext
12.00 noon

None
3.00 pm

Vespers
4.45 pm

Compline
7.25 pm

version of life worked out in a personal rule based on Saint Benedict's Rule. As members of the oblate family, they are united to the community and to their fellow oblates in mutual love and fellowship.

Oblates share in the community's worship by praying the Office, though not necessarily at the same times as at the abbey. The minimum is two Offices daily and if possible these are Lauds and Vespers. Eucharist: attendance at least once a week. Retreat: at least two days annually, at the abbey or elsewhere. Regular Prayer and *lectio*. Rule: to be read through at least annually.

The Chapel, Malling Abbey

Sisters of Charity

SC

Founded 1869

St Elizabeth's House
Longbrook Road
Plympton St Maurice
Plymouth
PL7 3NL

Tel: 01752 336112

A Community following the Rule of St Vincent de Paul and so committed to the service of those in need. Retreatants and guests are welcomed at the Mother House. The Sisters are involved in parish and mission work, chiefly in the Plymouth area, and they have a Mission House in Sunderland. The Community also has a nursing home in Plympton and a retreat house in Nevada in the USA.

MOTHER MARY THERESA
(Reverend Mother, assumed office 6 Jun 1987)
SR ELIZABETH MARY *(Assistant)*

Sr Muriel	Sr Philippa Margaret
Sr Rosalie	Sr Margaret Veronica
Sr Joan Vincent	Sr Mary Joseph
Sr Faith Mary	Sr Gabriel Margaret
Sr Theresa	Sr Clare *(priest)*
Sr Angela Mary	Sr Mary Patrick
Sr Rosamund	Sr Julian Hope
Sr Hilda Mary	Sr Mary Martha
Sr Faith Nicolette	Novices: 1

Guest and Retreat Facilities
ST ELIZABETH'S HOUSE   There is limited accommodation for retreatants. Two or three conducted retreats are held each year. Parish Groups and other organisations may use the facilities for Quiet Days. We also welcome individuals for private retreats and Quiet Days.

Oblates and Associates
The Community has a group of Oblates, associates and Friends, formed as a mutual supportive link. We do not provide a rule of life; instead we ask our Oblates and associates to add to their existing rule the daily use of the Community Prayer and the Holy Paraclete hymn. This hymn has been said three times a day by all Sisters from the beginning of the Community. Oblates are also invited to use one of the Daily Offices, thereby joining in spirit in the Divine Office of the Community. Oblates and Associates are encouraged to make an annual retreat, if possible at one of the Community houses. Friends support us by their prayers and annual subscription.

Morning Prayer
7.00 am

Holy Eucharist
8.00 am

Midday Office
12.00 noon

Vespers
5.00 pm

Compline
9.00 pm

Overseas
Convent & Retreat Centre, 701 Park Place,
PO Box 60818, Boulder City, Nevada 89006, USA
Tel: +1 702 293 4988

Sisterhood of the Epiphany

SE

Founded 1902

*All Hallows Convent
Ditchingham
Bungay
Suffolk
NR35 2DT*

Tel: 01986 892749

Founded for work in India as the Oxford Mission Sisterhood of the Epiphany, the sisters are now based at Ditchingham with the Community of All Hallows. The Christa Sevika Sangha, founded in 1970, which works in Barisal, Bangladesh, was under the guidance of the Sisterhood of the Epiphany from January 1970 until January 1993 (see overseas entries).

MOTHER WINIFRED
(Mother Superior, assumed office Jan 1997)

Sr Joan   Sr Florence   Sr Rosamund

Obituary
18 Jan 1997   Sr Muriel, aged 92 years,
                     professed 62 years

Community Publication
The Oxford Mission News, twice a year. Write to Oxford Mission, 1 Stridmore Cottages, Lee, Romsey, Hampshire SO51 9LF. *Tel: 01703 738652*

Community History
Brethren of the Epiphany, *A Hundred Years in Bengal*, ISPCK, Delhi, 1979.

Fellowship of the Epiphany
The Oxford Mission Fellowship of the Epiphany was founded in 1921 for friends of the Mission in India, Bangladesh, the British Isles and elsewhere.
Current membership: India: 40; Bangladesh: 21; British Isles: 46; elsewhere: 4.

Society of All Saints Sisters of the Poor

ASSP

Founded 1851

*All Saints Convent
St Mary's Road
Oxford
OX4 1RU*

*Tel: 01865 249127
Fax: 01865 726547*

*Registered
Charity No. 228383*

The Society has a residential home for the elderly, a children's hospice offering respite care for children with life-limiting illness, a drop-in centre for the homeless, an embroidery department and a small guest house. Sisters exercise a variety of individual ministries from both Oxford and All Saints House, Margaret Street.

SR HELEN
(Mother Superior, assumed office 29 Sep 1989)
SR FRANCES DOMINICA *(Assistant Superior)*

St John's Home	Helen House
(for the elderly)	*(children's hospice)*
St Mary's Road	37 Leopold Street
Oxford OX4 1QE	Oxford OX4 1QT
Tel: 01865 247725	*Tel: 01865 728251*

Embroidery Department	All Saints House
All Saints Convent	Margaret Street
St Mary's Road	London W1N 8LH
Oxford OX4 1RU	*Tel: 0171 637 7818*
Tel: 01865 248627	

Community Publication
New Venture, published annually in December. Order from the Society of All Saints.

Community History
Peter Mayhew, *All Saints: Birth & Growth of a Community*, ASSP, Oxford, 1987.

Community Wares
The Embroidery Department makes, repairs and remounts vestments, frontals etc.

Guest and Retreat Facilities
There is a small guest house with four rooms, and a small flatlet. Private retreats are possible when accommodation is free.

Associates
Those in sympathy with the aims of the community are invited to become Associates or Priest Friends.

Society of the Precious Blood

SPB

Founded 1905

Burnham Abbey
Lake End Road
Taplow
Maidenhead
Berkshire
SL6 OPW

Tel: 01628 604080

The Society is a contemplative community whose principle work is intercession. This life of prayer finds an outward expression in caring for guests who come, seeking an opportunity for quiet and reflection, help or counselling.

SISTER ELIZABETH MARY
(Reverend Mother, assumed office Jan 1998)

Sr Christine Mary	Sr Mary Philip
Sr Michael Mary	Sr Mary Peter
Sr Anne Mary	Sr Mary Benedict
Sr Mary S.Luke	Sr Jean Mary
Sr Raphael Mary	Sr Martha Mary
Sr Gabriel Mary	Sr Mary Andreas
Sr Margaret Mary	Sr Victoria Mary
Sr Mary S. John	Sr Miriam Mary
Sr Agatha Mary	Sr Agnes Mary
Sr Mary Bernard	Sr Mary Joseph
Sr Dorothy Mary	Sr Angela Mary
Sr Jane Mary	Sr Mary Francis
Sr Mary Laurence	*Novices:* 1

Obituary
29 Oct 1997   Sr Veronica Mary, aged 86 years, professed 47 years

Other UK Houses
St Pega's Hermitage, Peakirk, Peterborough PE6 7NP
Tel: 01733 252219

Lauds
5.50 am   (6.10 am Sun)

Matins
7.15 am

Terce & Eucharist
9.00 am

Angelus & Sext
12.00 noon

Quiet Time
1.15 pm - 3.00 pm

Vespers
5.30 pm

Compline
8.30 pm

Community Publication
Newsletter, yearly at Christmas. Write to the Abbey.

Community History
Sr Felicity Mary SPB, *Mother Millicent Mary of the Will of God*, Macmillan, London, 1968.

Community wares
Cards, rosaries, holding crosses.

Guest and Retreat Facilities
There is a small guest house for individual (unconducted) retreats.

Companions and Oblates

Companions and Oblates of the Society are Christians who wish to identify themselves with the life and aims of the Society and to share in its worship and intercession as fully as possible according to the varying circumstances of their lives.

The Chapel, Burnham Abbey

Society of the Sacred Cross

SSC

Founded 1914
(Chichester);
re-established in 1923
(Wales)

Tymawr Convent
Lydart
Monmouth
Gwent
NP5 4RN

Tel: 01600 860244
Tel. bookings:
6.45 pm - 8 pm only
except Fri & Sun

Morning Prayer
7.00 am

Terce
8.45 am

Eucharist
12.00 noon

Evening Prayer
5.30 pm

Compline
8.30 pm

The community, part of the Anglican Church in Wales, lives a monastic, contemplative life of prayer based on silence, solitude and learning to live together, under vows of poverty, chastity and obedience, with a modern rule, Cistercian in spirit. At the heart of our corporate life is the Eucharist with the daily Office and other times of shared prayer spanning the day. All services are open to the public and we are often joined by members of the neighbourhood in addition to our visitors. Our common life includes study, recreation and work in the house and extensive grounds. It is possible for women and men, married or single, to experience our life of prayer by living alongside the community for periods longer than the usual guest stay. Hospitality is an important part of our life at Tymawr and guests are most welcome. We also organise and sponsor occasional lectures and programmes of study for those who wish to find or develop the life of the spirit in their own circumstances. The community is dedicated to the crucified and risen Lord as the focus of its life and the source of the power to live it.

MOTHER GILLIAN MARY
(Reverend Mother, assumed office 1986)
SR ANNE & SR MARY JEAN (Deputy Leaders)

Sr Jeanne   Sr Heylin Columba*
Sr Clare   Sr Mary Janet
Sr Rosemary   Sr Susan
Sr Paula   Sr Cara Mary
Sr Veronica Ann   Sr Joan
Sr Lorna Francis*   Novices: 1

*Living the contemplative life away from Tymawr.

Community Publication
Tymawr Newsletter, yearly at Advent. Write to the above address.

Guest and Retreat Facilities
The community offers facilities for individual guests and small groups. There are five rooms (one double) in the guest wing of the Main House for full board. Michaelgarth, the self-catering guest house, offers facilities for individuals or groups (five singles and two doubles). Individuals may have private retreats with guidance from a member of the community. The community also organises a varied programme of retreats, quiet days and pilgrimage days on particular themes through the

year. Please write with a stamped addressed envelope for details.

Oblates and Associates
There are thirty-eight Oblates, living in their own houses, each having a personal Rule sustaining their life of prayer. Three Companion brothers meet regularly at Tymawr under a Rule appropriate to their ministries, based on the SSC Rule. There are sixty-three Women Associates and forty-eight Men Associates with a simple commitment, who are part of the extended family.

Tymawr Convent Chapel

*Walking shakes thoughts
from the head
into the guts,
into the bloodstream.*

Donald Nicholl

Society of the Sacred Mission

SSM

Founded 1893

*1 Linford Lane
Milton Keynes
MK15 9DL*

*Tel & Fax:
01908 234546*

The Society is a means of uniting the devotion of ordinary people, using it in the service of the Church. It is made up of professed brothers: men, who after two or three years training as novices, profess their intention of remaining in the Society for life. Members of the Society share a common life of prayer and fellowship in a variety of educational, pastoral and community activities in England, Australia, Japan, Lesotho, Papua New Guinea and South Africa.

CHRISTOPHER MYERS
(Director, assumed office Aug 1996)

Paul Hume	Dunstan McKee
Alban Perkins	Ralph Martin
Clement Mullenger	Peter Story
Laurence Eyers	Thomas Brown
John Lewis	Andrew Muramatsu
Austin Masters	Jonathan Ewer
Frank Green	Rodney Hart
Anthony Perry	Edmund Wheat
Henry Arkell	Michael Lapsley
Hilary Greenwood	Matthew Dowsey
Douglas Brown	Colin Griffiths
Andrew Longley	William Nkomo
David Wells	Gary Askey
Gordon Holroyd	Robert Stretton
Francis Horner	Roderick McDougall
Hector Lee	Steven Haws

*Novices, Southern Province: 3
Postulants, Southern Province: 2*

Community Publication
Sacred Mission (newsletter of the Southern Province):
The Editor, St Michael's Priory, 75 Watson's Road, Diggers Rest, Victoria 3427, Australia

SSM News (newsletter of the Province of Europe):
The Secretary, SSM Newsletter, 1 Linford Lane, Milton Keynes MK15 9DL

Community History
Alistair Mason, *SSM: History of the Society of the Sacred Mission*, Canterbury Press Norwich, 1993.

Province of Europe

St Antony's Priory
Claypath
Durham DH1 1QT
Tel: 0191 384 3747
Fax: 0191 384 4939

House of the Sacred Mission
90 Vassall Road
Kennington
London SW9 6JA
Tel: 0171 582 2040
Fax: 0171 582 6640

Southern Province

St John's Priory
14 St John's Street
Adelaide
SOUTH AUSTRALIA 5000
Tel: +61 8 8223 1014
Fax: +61 8 8223 2764

Newton Theological College
PO Box 162
Popondetta
Ora Province
PAPUA NEW GUINEA

St Michael's Priory
75 Watson's Road
Diggers Rest
Victoria 3427
AUSTRALIA
Tel: +61 3 9740 1618
Fax: +61 3 9740 0007

Priory of the Sacred Mission
PO Box 1579
Maseru 100
LESOTHO

St Antony's Priory, Claypath, Durham

Society of St Francis

SSF

Founded 1921

Hilfield Friary
Dorchester
Dorset
DT2 7BE

Tel: 01300 341345
Fax: 01300 341293

E-Mail:
HilfieldSSF@aol.com

Morning Prayer
7.00 am   (7.30 am Sun)

Midday Prayer
12.00 noon

Eucharist
12.15 pm
(8.30 am Sun,
6.15 pm Thu)

Evening Prayer
5.45 pm (5.00 pm Sun)

Night Prayer
9.30 pm (8.30 pm Thu)

The Society of St Francis has diverse origins in a number of Franciscan groups which drew together during the 1930s to found one Franciscan Society. SSF in its widest definition includes First Order friars and sisters (CSF), Second Order sisters (OSC) and a Third Order. The First Order life exists in many forms, but common to all is the life of prayer, Office and Eucharist and a commitment to the service of the poor. The Brothers' work includes retreats, counselling and missions, being a prayerful presence in inner city areas, the provision of food and lodging for wayfarers, and parish work. SSF brothers work in Europe, America, Australasia and the Pacific.

DANIEL
(Minister General, assumed office Jul 1997)

European Province
DAMIAN
(Minister Provincial, assumed office Jul 1991)
SAMUEL (Assistant Minister)

Aidan	Harry
Alan	Hubert
Alan Michael	Hugo
Alistair	James Anthony
Amos	James William
Angelo	Jason
Anselm	John Francis
Arnold	Jonathan
Austin	Jude
Benedict	Julian
Benjamin	Kentigern John
Bernard	Kevin
Bruce Paul	Malcolm
Christian	Martin
David	Matthew
David Francis	Michael
David Jardine	Nathanael
David Stephen	Paschal
Desmond Alban	Paul
Dominic Christopher	Paul Anthony
Donald	Peter Douglas
Edmund	Philip
Edward	Philip Bartholomew
Geoffrey	Ramon
Giles	Raphael
Gordon	Raymond Christian
Gregory	Reginald

Robbie Asaph
Robert Coombes
Roger Alexander
Ronald
Seraphim
Simeon Christopher

Thomas Anthony
Tristam
Vincent
Wilfrid

Novices: 8

UK Houses

The Friary
Alnmouth
Alnwick
Northumberland NE66 3NJ
Tel: 01665 830213
E-Mail: GenSec SSF@aol.com

St Damian's House
Flat 1
184 Ley Hill Farm Road
Birmingham B31 1UQ
Tel: 0121 411 1276

Saint Francis House
14/15 Botolph Lane
Cambridge CB2 3RD
Tel: 01223 353903 & 321576

The Little Portion
111/2 Lothian Road
Edinburgh EH3 9AN
Tel: 0131 228 3077

Alverna
110 Ellesmere Road
Gladstone Park
London NW10 1JS
Tel & Fax: 0181 452 7285

16 Dalserf Street
Barrowfield
Glasgow G31 4AS
Tel: 0141 550 1202

St Mary-at-the-Cross
Glasshampton
Shrawley
Worcestershire WR6 6TQ
Tel: 01299 896345

Holy Trinity House
Orsett Terrace
Paddington
London W2 6AH
Tel: 0171 723 9735

House of the Divine Compassion
42 Balaam Street
Plaistow
London E13 8AQ
Tel: 0171 476 5189

10 Halcrow Street
Stepney
London E1 2EP
Tel: 0171 247 6233

Community Publications
franciscan, three times a year. Write to the Subscriptions Secretary at Hilfield Friary.
Books available from Hilfield Friary book shop include:
The Daily Office SSF: A version of Celebrating Common Prayer, £14.50 + £2 p&p.

Community History
Petà Dunstan, *This Poor Sort: A History of the European Province of the Society of Saint Francis,* DLT, 1997, £19.95 + £2 p&p.

Community Wares
Hilfield Friary shop has friary-made prayer stools, 'Freeland' cards & traidcraft goods

Guest and Retreat Facilities

ALNMOUTH   The Friary has twelve rooms (including one twin-bedded) for men or women guests. Some conducted retreats are held each year and individually-guided retreats are available on request.

GLASSHAMPTON   The guest accommodation, available to both men and women, comprises five rooms. Groups can visit for the day, but may not exceed fifteen people.

HILFIELD   The Guest House, for men and women guests, was refurbished early in 1998 and contains eleven single rooms plus a double room which has wheelchair access. The friary is closed Mondays, so guests may stay from Tuesday to Sunday afternoon.

Third Order

The Third Order of the Society of St Francis consists of men and women, ordained and lay, married or single, who believe that God is calling them to live out their Franciscan vocation in the world, living in their own homes and doing their own jobs. Living under a rule of life, with the help of a spiritual director, members (called tertiaries) encourage one another in living and witnessing to Christ, being organised in Regions and Areas to enable regular meetings to be held. There are some 1800 tertiaries in the European Province of this world-wide Order, with a Minister General and five Ministers Provincial to cover the relevant Provinces.

Information about the Third Order (often called Tertiaries) can be obtained from: The Minister Provincial TSSF, Lochside, Lochwinnoch, Renfrewshire PA12 4JH.

Companions

Companions are individual Christians who wish to associate themselves with the Society through prayer, friendship and in seeking to live the spirit of the Gospel in the way of St Francis. For more information about becoming a Companion contact: The Secretary for Companions, Hilfield Friary, Dorchester, Dorset DT2 7BE.

The Courtyard, Hilfield Friary

American Province
JUSTUS RICHARD
(Minister Provincial, assumed office May 1993)

Anthony Michael
Antonio Sato
Clark Berge
Derek
Dominic
Dunstan
James Edward

Jason Robert
John George
Jon Bankert
Robert Hugh
Thomas

Novices 2

Little Portion Friary, PO Box 399, Mount Sinai, NY 11766/0399, USA
Tel: +1 516 473 0533; Fax: +1 516 473 9434; E:Mail: bankert@li.net

St Elizabeth's Friary, 1474 Bushwick Ave, Brooklyn, NY 11207, USA
Tel: +1 718 455 5963; Fax: +1 718 443 3437

San Damiano, 573 Dolores St, San Francisco, CA 94110, USA
Tel :+1 415 861 1372; Fax: +1 415 861 7952
(Minister Provincial, Tel & fax: +1 415 703 0953; E-Mail: Justus_VanHouten@ecunet.org)

Australia/New Zealand Province
COLIN WILFRED
(Minister Provincial, assumed office Jul 1997)

Alfred Boonkong
Brian
Christopher John
Damian Kenneth
Donald Campbell
Francis
Leo Anthony

Masseo
Moses Lonsdale
Noel Thomas
Peter Christian
William

Novices: 3

The Hermitage, PO Box 46, Stroud, NSW 2425, AUSTRALIA
Tel: +61 2 4994 5372; Fax: +61 2 4994 5527; E-Mail: ssfstrd@midac.com.au

The Friary, 115 Cornwall St, Annerley, Brisbane, Qd 4103, AUSTRALIA
Tel: +61 7 3391 3915; Fax: +61 7 3391 3916

St Francis Friary, PO Box 89-085, Torbay, Auckland, NEW ZEALAND
Tel: +64 9 473 2605; Fax: +64 9 473 2606; E-Mail: damiankssf@xtra.co.nz

Pacific Islands Province: Papua New Guinea Region
CLIFTON HENRY
(Deputy Minister, Papua New Guinea Region)

Ananias Korina	Lester
Andrew	Nathanael Gari
Anthony	Oswald
Benjamin Tapio	Peter Kevin
Bray Ungaia	Philip Etobae
Cecil Okun	Selwyn Suma
George Alfred	Smith Tovebae
Gilson Kira	Timothy Joseph
Hugh	Walter
Jerry Ross	Wilson Bosa
Laurence Hauje	*Novices:* 15

St Mary of the Angels Friary, Haruro, PO Box 78, Popondetta, Oro Province

Katerada, PO Box 78, Popondetta, Oro Province

Dipoturu, PO Box 78, Popondetta, Oro Province

Douglas House, PO Box 3411, Lae, Morobe Province

c/o St Francis Church, PO Box 576, Goroka, Eastern Highlands Province

Pacific Islands Province: Solomon Islands Region
ANDREW MANU
(Deputy Minister, Solomon Islands Region)

Athanasius	Patrick Kiko
Bartholomew Maesiwou	Patteson Kwa'ai
Colin	Peter Ambiofa
Comins Romano	Robert Briel
David Raurau	Samson Amoni
Dudley Palmer	Samson Siho
Gabriel Maelesi	Selwyn Kaekae
George Huinodi	Shadrack Mamaone
Josiah Waifu	Shedrich Iru
Layban Kwanafia	Stanley Sinewala
Manasseh Birahu	Zachariah Talanitei
Matthias Kaefiu	
Nicholas Tai	*Novices:* 16

Patteson House, PO Box 519, Honiara   *Tel: +677 22386*
Regional Office, Tel & fax: + 677 25810; E-Mail: Francis@welkam.solomon.com.sb

La Verna Friary, Hautambu, PO Box 519, Honiara

The Friary, PO Box 7, Auki, Malaita Province

San Damiano Friary, Diocese of Hanuato'o, Kira Kira, Makira Ulawa Province

Society of St John the Evangelist

SSJE

Founded 1866

*St Edward's House
22 Great College Street
Westminster
London
SW1P 3QA*

Tel: 0171 222 9234

*Mattins
7.00 am*

*Eucharist
7.30 am
(8.00 am Sun)*

*Terce
9.45 am*

*Sext
12.45 pm*

*Evensong
6.30 pm*

*Compline
9.30 pm*

The Chapter of the Society of St John the Evangelist, in the discussions which led to consideration of a wider Fellowship (see below), also agreed to close the old-style noviciate, and not train any aspirants specifically for SSJE as it has been known, and as it is still known today. It was agreed the training should look towards a new community, which will probably wish to call itself The Society of St John (although it has the freedom not to do so). Novices would be called 'Seekers - associate members', and those in the equivalent of First Vows 'Internal Oblates', these all being legally recognised terms within the constitution of SSJE. There are now two Internal Oblates and one Seeker.

The active life of the newcomers enables those activities for which the older members are trained, and which they are still able to do, to go on without hindrance. Thus, in London, many days are still filled with retreats, quiet days, parish conferences, groups coming for prayer (a group concerned for Africa, MP's wives, business people in discussion), the midweek Eucharist, and individuals visiting for a variety of reasons. In Oxford, despite limitations, individuals are welcomed and a varied ministry goes on. At Haywards Heath, those resident are endeavouring to recreate a ministry for retreat, prayer, etc., although now without the guiding hand in residence of Fr Slade.

But alongside, there is also new work and outreach. Each new person is encouraged to use their own gifts much more: counselling, mission to senior citizens, liturgy, working for healing, mission to other local Christians, and to people met in the street, especially those of other nationalities. Work continues with artists, people with dyslexia and ME, and some abuse-counselling. The Society thus tries to seek the will of God for its present and future life, and discern what the Church shall require of it.

FR JAMES NATERS
(Superior General, assumed office 1991)
FR ALAN GRAINGE *(Assistant Superior)*

Fr Herbert Slade	Br Gerald Perkins
Br Anselm Chiverton	Br Adrian Tate
Fr Alan Bean	
Fr Stuart Lennard	*Internal Oblates*
Fr David Campbell	Fr Nicholas Wickham
Fr Peter Palmer	Br James Simon
Fr Alan Cotgrove	*Seekers: 1*

Obituaries

12 Feb 1997   Fr Mark Gibbard, aged 86 years, member of SSJE since 1943

21 Jun 1997   Fr Arthur Phalo, aged 71 years, member of SSJE since 1960

Community Publication

Newsletter, published monthly, is edited by Graham Johnson, Launde Abbey, East Norton, Leicester, LE7 9XB. It goes out to two hundred or more members and potential members of the Fellowship, as well as to Religious Communities and to friends, on an ever-growing mailing list.

Guest and Retreat Facilities

ST EDWARD'S HOUSE   Three conducted retreats are held each year; and there are Quarterly Quiet Days. Individual retreatants are welcomed and there are also facilities for Quiet Days.

THE OXFORD PRIORY also has a room available for retreatants.

Other UK Houses

The Anchorhold, Paddockhall Rd, Haywards Heath, Sussex RH16 1HN
Tel: 01444 452468

The Priory, 228 Iffley Rd, Oxford OX4 1SE
Tel: 01865 248116

The (new) Fellowship of St John

In 1994, a working party, gathered under the convenorship of Fr Alan Cotgrove, was asked by Chapter to strengthen the ties between the Society and the old Fellowship. During three years of discussions, the idea of a wider Fellowship of St John emerged, incorporating the professed members of the Society as one of its parts. This new Fellowship has its own new logo. From the Working Party - or Core Group, as it became known - a team of seven people have formed a management group to develop this new Fellowship.

Two major groups flourish: in London, under the Revd Ann Gurney, and in the South, under Dr Hilary Knight. 'Things are also happening' in the East Midlands and the Potteries. The rest of the country, as well as twenty or so members in Australia, Canada, Germany (twinned with the Ecumenical Community of the Holy Cross), New Zealand (including one oblate), and South Africa, are in direct contact with the Contacts Officer at St Edward's House. Full lists, as well as area lists, have been sent to members for private intercession. An Office Book is due for publication in the near future, together with a Manual.

Overseas

The Society in North America is independent (see overseas section for addresses), but in very close touch with the Society in England. The American SSJE has a noviciate and is growing in numbers. The members are engaged in retreat work, in parish missions, in running seminars and in individual formation. It is also responsible for the large continuing St Augustine's camp for boys.

*Society of
St Margaret
(Aberdeen)*

Saint Margaret's Convent, Aberdeen, is one of the autonomous Houses which constitute the Society of St Margaret, founded by John Mason Neale. The Community is at present engaged in hospital chaplaincy, pastoral and retreat work, and has limited holiday accommodation.

SSM

MOTHER VERITY MARGARET
(Mother Superior, assumed office 6 Mar 1965)
Sr Mary Thecla
Sr Columba
Sr Mary Joan

Founded 1864

*St Margaret's Convent
17 Spital
Aberdeen
AB24 3HT*

Community Publication
Oremus, annually in Advent. Write to the Mother Superior. There is no fixed subscription, but donations towards stationery and postage are welcome.

Tel: 01224 632648

Community History
Sr Catherine Louise SSM, *The Planting of the Lord: The History of the Society of Saint Margaret in England, Scotland & the USA;* privately published, 1995.

*Matins
7.30 am*

*Terce
9.00 am*

*Midday Office
12.45 pm*

*Vespers
5.30 pm*

*Compline
8.30 pm*

*Mass
12.00 noon Sun, Thu &
Sat
9.30 am Mon & Fri
7.30 am Tue
5.30 pm Wed*

St Margaret's Convent, Aberdeen

Society of St Margaret (East Grinstead)

SSM

Saint Margaret's Convent, East Grinstead, is one of the autonomous Houses which constitute the Society of St Margaret founded by John Mason Neale. The Sisters' work is the worship of God, expressed in their life of prayer and service. They welcome visitors to a guest house, a retreat house and a conference centre, Neale House, and are involved in spiritual direction, counselling and parish work. At Chiswick they care for elderly women in a nursing home and a guest house. There are two branch houses in Sri Lanka.

MOTHER RAPHAEL MARY
(Mother Superior, assumed office 9 Feb 1985)
SR CYNTHIA CLARE *(Assistant Superior)*

Founded 1855

*St Margaret's Convent
St John's Road
East Grinstead
West Sussex
RH19 3LE*

Tel: 01342 323497

Sr Mary Joan
Sr Felicity
Sr Edna
Sr Rosemary
Sr Rosamond
Sr Winifred
Sr Hazel
Sr Sophia
Sr Lorna Mary
Sr Letitia
Sr Mary Joseph

Sr Mary Michael
Sr Rita Margaret
Sr Eleanor
Sr Jennifer Anne
Sr Lucy
Sr Barbara
Sr Mary Paul
Sr Elizabeth
Sr Mary Clare
Sr Sarah

*Matins
6.45 am
(7.30 am Sun,
7.20 am Thu)*

*Eucharist
7.20 am
(9.30 am Sun & Thu)*

*Litany of the Holy Name
8.25 am*

*Midday Office
12.45 pm*

*Vespers
5.05 pm (4.50 pm Sun)*

*Compline
8.35 pm*

Obituary
9 Jun 1997   Sr Osyth, aged 87 years, professed 52 years

Neale House Conference Centre
Moat Rd, East Grinstead, West Sussex RH19 3LB
Tel: 01342 312552

St Mary's Convent & Nursing Home
Burlington Lane, Chiswick, London W4 2QF
Tel: 0181 994 4641

Community Publication
St Margaret's Chronicle, three times a year. Write to the Editor at St Margaret's Convent.

Community History
Sr Catherine Louise SSM, *The Planting of the Lord: The History of the Society of Saint Margaret in England, Scotland & the USA*; privately published, 1995.

Guest and Retreat Facilities
There are fourteen beds, primarily for individual retreats. Day retreatants are welcome both as individuals and in groups of up to twenty people. There are conducted Quiet days once a month for up to twenty people. Some Sisters are available for support in these retreats.

Associates
Associates observe a simple Rule, share in the life of prayer and dedication of the community, and are welcomed at all SSM convents.

Semi-autonomous houses overseas
The Sisters run a Retreat House, a Children's Home (mainly for those orphaned in the ongoing civil strife), a Hostel for young women, a Home for elderly people, and are involved in parish work, church embroidery and wafer baking.

SR LUCY AGNES
(Sister Superior)
Sr Edith
Sr Miriam
Sr Jane Margaret
Sr Maria Margaret
Sr Mary Christine
Sr Chandrani

St Margaret's Convent
157 St Michael's Rd, Polwatte,
Colombo 3, SRI LANKA

St John's Home, 133 Galle Rd,
Moratuwa, SRI LANKA

The Convent, East Grinstead

Society of St Margaret (Haggerston)

SSM

Founded 1866

St Saviour's Priory
18 Queensbridge Road
Haggerston, London
E2 8NS

Tel: 0171 739 9976
Tel: (Revd Mother and
fax) 0171 739 6775

S aint Saviour's Priory is one of the autonomous Houses which constitute the Society of St Margaret founded by John Mason Neale. The Community pursues the 'mixed' life of prayer and work, seeking to respond to some of the needs that arise in East London. The Office is four-fold and the Eucharist is offered daily. The Sisters' outreach to the local community includes: working as staff members in various parishes; supporting issues of justice and racial equality; working in schools and with young people; the homeless; those with HIV/AIDS; the sexually abused; hospital chaplaincy; retreats and individual spiritual direction. The Sisters are also called to a ministry of welcome: sharing their community building and resources of worship and space with individuals and groups.

SR ELIZABETH CRAWFORD
(Reverend Mother, assumed office Feb 1992)
SR ANNA HUSTON *(Assistant Superior)*

Sr Natalie Bryan	Sr Moira Jones
Sr Beatrice Follows	Sr Mary Michael (Lilian) Stokes
Sr Susan Harris	Sr Helen Loder *(priest)*
Sr Pauline (Mary) Hardcastle	Sr Enid Margaret Jealous
Sr Frances (Claire) Carter	Sr Pamela Radford
Sr Joyce Anderson	Sr June Atkinson
Sr Marjorie Kelly	Sr Sue Makin
Sr Monica Popper	Sr Judith Blackburn

Obituary
9 Aug 1997   Sr Dorothy Mary Young, aged 93 years, professed 61 years

Morning Prayer
7.15 am (8.00 am Sun)
followed by Eucharist
(12.15 pm Eucharist
on major feasts
& 12.30 pm on Sun)

Midday Office
12.45 pm

Evening Prayer
5.00 pm

Night Prayer
8.30 pm

Community Publication
The Orient, yearly. Write to The Orient Secretary at St Saviour's Priory. Brochures about the Community are available at any time on request.

Community History
Memories of a Sister of S. Saviour's Priory, A.R. Mowbray, 1904.
A Hundred Years in Haggerston, published by St Saviour's Priory, 1966.
Sr Catherine Louise SSM, *The Planting of the Lord: The History of the Society of Saint Margaret in England, Scotland & the USA*; privately published, 1995.

Community Wares
Traidcraft, cards, books and religious items are all for sale.

Guest and Retreat Facilities
Six single and two double rooms for individual guests. Excellent facilities for non-residential group meetings.

Associates and Friends
Associates make a long term commitment to the Society of St Margaret, following a Rule of Life and helping the Community where possible. An Associate of one SSM house is an Associate of all the houses. There are regular quiet days for Associates who are kept in touch with community developments.

Friends of St Saviour's Priory commit themselves to a year of mutual support and friendship and are invited to regular events throughout the year.

St Saviour's Priory, Haggerston

Society of St Margaret (Walsingham)

SSM

founded 1855

(Walsingham Priory founded 1955)

The Priory of Our Lady
Walsingham
Norfolk
NR22 6ED

Tel: (Code) 01328
820340 (Revd Mother)
820901 (Sisters &
guests)
Fax: 01328 820899

Readings & Morning
Prayer
7.00 am (6.30 am Thu)

Mass
9.30 am
(7.15 am Thu,
10.00 am Sun)

Midday Office
12.45 pm

Vespers
5.00 pm

Compline
8.45 pm

In January 1994, the Priory of Our Lady at Walsingham reverted to being an autonomous house of the Society of St Margaret. The Sisters' daily life is centred on the Eucharist and the daily Office, from which flows their growing involvement in the ministry of healing, and reconciliation in the Shrine, the local parishes and the wider Church. They welcome guests for short periods of rest, relaxation and retreat, and are available to pilgrims and visitors. They also work in the Education Department in the Shrine.

MOTHER MARY TERESA
(Reverend Mother, assumed office 29 Jan 1994)

Sr Julian	Sr Jean Mary
Sr Joan Michael	Sr Francis Anne
Sr Christina Mary	Sr Wendy Renate
Sr Mary Kathleen	Sr Phyllis
Sr Alma Mary	Novices: 4

Obituaries

27 Jan 1997	Sr Angela, aged 90 years, professed 62 years
5 Aug 1997	Sr Clare, aged 87 years, professed 46 years

Community Publication
Yearly Christmas letter. Write to The Priory.

Community History
Sr Catherine Louise SSM, *The Planting of the Lord: The History of the Society of Saint Margaret in England, Scotland & the USA*; privately published.

Community Wares
Cards (re-cycled) and embroidered; books; religious objects (statues etc.)

Guest and Retreat Facilities
Available from Easter 1998.

Associates
There are associates and friends: for information apply to Reverend Mother.

Society of the Sisters of Bethany

SSB

Founded 1866

7 Nelson Road
Southsea
Hampshire
PO5 2AR

Tel: 01705 833498

By prayer and activity, the Sisters seek to share in the work of reconciling the divided Churches of Christendom and the whole world. By simplicity of life-style, the Sisters try to identify with those for whom they share in Christ's work of intercession in the power of the Holy Spirit. The work of the Sisters includes giving hospitality for those seeking spiritual or physical refreshment and arranging retreats and quiet days in their houses. They also extend their work to counselling, spiritual direction and helping in parishes. From time to time they are engaged in missions and cathedral chaplaincy work. Their noviciate is at Hindhead.

MOTHER GWENYTH
(Reverend Mother, assumed office 1 Nov 1994)
SR CHRISTINE ALICE *(Assistant Superior)*

Sr Janet	Sr Elspeth
Sr Margaret Faith	Sr Florence May
Sr Elisabeth Julian	Sr Ann Patricia
Sr Christina Mary	Sr Constance Mary
Sr Margaret May	Sr Hilary
Sr Grace Ninian	Sr Mary Joy
Sr Marjorie Mary	Sr Rita-Elizabeth
Sr Katherine Maryel	Sr Teresa Mary
Sr Ruth Etheldreda	*Novices:* 1

House of Bethany, Tilford Rd, Hindhead, Surrey GU26 6RB
Tel: 01428 604578 (house closing Dec 1998)

Mattins
7.00 am

Mass
7.45 am

Terce
9.00 am

Midday Office
12.00 noon

Vespers
5.00 pm

Compline
8.45 pm

Guest and Retreat Facilities
HINDHEAD: ten bedrooms. Groups of ten people can be accommodated, with a conductor.
SOUTHSEA: four guest rooms. Individual retreatants can be accommodated.

Community wares
Cards.

Associates
The associates are a body of close friends who unite their life of prayer to that of the community and who are accepted as members of an extended community family. They live in their own homes and accept a simple rule of life which is the expression of a shared concern to love and serve God and one another after the example of Martha, Mary and Lazarus.

Anglican Religious Communities

outside the UK

It is hoped that,
in any future edition of the Year Book,
it may be possible to expand this section.

Christa Sevika Sangha (Handmaids of Christ)

CSS

Founded 1970

The Community was founded in 1970 and was under the care of the Sisterhood of the Epiphany until 1993. The Sevikas supervise boys' and girls' hostels and a play-centre for small children. They also help in St Gabriel's School and supervise St Mary's Asroi (Home) at Barisal.

SR SUSILA
(Mother Foundress)

Sr Ruth	Sr Margaret
Sr Jharna	Sr Kalyani
Sr Sobha	
Sr Agnes	*Novices:* 4
Sr Dorothy	*Postulants:* 1

Jobarpar, Barisal Division, Uz Agailjhara 8240
BANGLADESH

Oxford Mission, Bogra Rd, PO Box 21, Barisal 8200
BANGLADESH

Community of the Good Shepherd

CGS

Founded 1920

The CGS Sisters in Malaysia were formerly a part of the Community of the Companions of Jesus the Good Shepherd in the UK. They became an autonomous community in 1978. Their Rule is based on that of St Augustine and their ministry is mainly parish work.

Sr Oi Chin
Sr Margaret Lin-Din

POB 17, 90007, Sandakan, Sabah, East MALAYSIA

Community of St John the Baptist

CSJB

Founded 1852

SR SUZANNE ELIZABETH
(Mother Superior, assumed office Nov 1983)
SR BARBARA JEAN *(priest) (Assistant Superior)*

Sr Margaret Helena
Sr Laura Katharine
Sr Mary Lynne
Sr Deborah Frances
Sr Margo Elizabeth
Novices: 1

PO Box 240, Mendham, NJ 07945, USA
Tel: +1 201 543 4641; Fax: +1 201 543 0327

Community Publication
Newsletter, three times a year. Write to the Convent.

Congregation of the Sisters of the Visitation of our Lady

CSVL

Founded 1964

In the early 1960s, three young women accompanied a Holy Name Sister to Hetune, a site near Popondetta in the then Northern Province, to test their vocation to the Religious Life. The group became known as the Community of the Visitation and for the next twenty years remained concentrated at Hetune, making two attempts at opening further communities, first at Madang, then at Dotura.

The Congregation, on the basis of its spirituality springing from the life and discipleship of Our Lady, focuses its apostolate on the family which it undertakes through complementary ministries of hospitality within its own community houses and visiting in family homes and centres of family activity.

SR ANN *(Guardian)*
Professed Sisters: 11

Convent of the Visitation, Hetune, Box 18, Popondetta
Oro Province, PAPUA NEW GUINEA

House of Our Lady of Reconciliation
Box 1547, Goroka 441, Eastern Highlands Province
PAPUA NEW GUINEA
Tel: +675 732 3190; Fax (Church): +675 732 1214

Order of St Benedict

Bartonville

OSB

Founded 1985

The Community was founded on 15 August 1985 at San Juan in Puerto Rico, as a Spanish (Anglican) Benedictine house. They have no active apostolate, concentrating upon the Divine Office, daily mass and praying for the Church. What work they do for the Church is done within the monastery. Late in 1996, the community moved from Puerto Rico to Bartonville, Illinois. They have been affiliated to Alton Abbey in the UK since 1995.

RT REVD DOM J ALBERTO MORALES
(Abbot, elected 1991)
VERY REVD DOM TREVOR RHODES *(Prior)*

Revd Dom Lewis Gonzalez
Revd Dom Harold Camacho
Dom Pedro Augustino Escabi

Abbey of Saint Benedict, 7561 West Lancaster Road
Bartonville, Illinois 51607, USA
Tel: +1 309 633 0057; Fax: +1 309 633 0058

Order of St Benedict

St Mark's Priory, Camperdown

OSB

Founded 1975

Benedictine Monastery
PO Box 111
Camperdown
Victoria 3260

Tel: +61 3 559 32348

The community was founded in Melbourne in 1975. In 1980, having adopted the Rule of Saint Benedict, the monks moved to the country town of Camperdown. The community lives a contemplative life with the emphasis on the life of prayer and work that forms the Benedictine ethos. In 1993, the Chapter decided to endeavour to establish a mixed community of monks and nuns. To this end, two nuns came from Malling Abbey in the UK and one has transferred her stability to Camperdown.

THE VERY REVD DOM MICHAEL KING
(Prior, installed 21 Mar 1980)
SISTER MARY PHILIP BLOORE *(Sub-Prior)*
Dom Placid Lawson
Oblate Sister Mary John Winterbotham
Postulants: 2

Community Publication
Annual newsletter at Christmas.

Oblates
There is a small group of clerics and lay people who form the Oblates of the Community following the Benedictine life according to their particular status.

Order of St Benedict

Pusan

OSB

Founded 1993

The Order was founded in September 1993 at the request of the Most Revd Bundo Kim, Bishop of Pusan, Korea. It follows the Rule of St Benedict. The Benedictine spirit is expressed in the work of prayer: the Divine Office, meditation, spiritual reading and silence. The Order has no specific work, but is open to all missions and works of the Church in Korea, as the Sisters' abilities permit.

SR HANNAH
(Sister-in-charge)

Sr Martha
Sr Michaela

810-1 Baekrok-ri, Habuk-myon, Yangsan-shi, Kyongnam-do, 626-860 KOREA
Tel: +82 51 523 841560

Society of the Holy Cross (SHC)

Seoul

Founded 1925

3 Chong-dong, Jung-ku, Seoul 100-120, KOREA

Tel: +82 2 735 7832 (& 3478)
Fax: +82 2 736 5028

The community was started by the Community of St Peter, Woking. The Sisters base their spirituality on a form of the Augustinian Rule. Their activities include working in parishes, retreats, running homes for the elderly and those with learning difficulties, counselling and teaching, making vestments, wafers and communion wine, and running women's projects.

MOTHER EDITH
(Leader, assumed office 1 Jan 1996)
SR MARIA AGNES *(Deputy Leader)*

Sr Tabitha	Sr Angela
Sr Maria	Sr Monica Alma
Sr Esther	Sr Martha Joanna
Sr Monica	Sr Helena Elizabeth
Sr Phoebe Anne	Sr Theresa
Sr Cecilia	Sr Grace
Sr Maria Helen	Sr Lucy Juliana
Sr Etheldreda	Sr Anna Frances
Sr Aeun	Sr Susanna
Sr Catherine	Sr Lucy Edward
Sr Maria Clare	Sr Lucy Jemma
Sr Pauline	

Community Publication
Holy Cross Newsletter, published quarterly (in Korean).

Addresses of some other Communities Outside the UK

Houses belonging to communities also based in the UK are listed under that community in the previous pages of this Directory.

Key: ♂ men, ♀ women

AFRICA

♀ ♂ **Chita Che Zita Rinoyera** (CZR)
CZR Convent, St Augustine's Mission, PO Penhalonga, Mutare, ZIMBABWE

♀ **Community of the Blessed Lady Mary** (CBLM)
Shearly Cripps Children's Home, PB600E, Harare, ZIMBABWE

♂ **Community of the Divine Compassion** (CDC)
St Augustine's Mission, PO Penhalonga, Mutare, ZIMBABWE

♀ ♂ **Community of the Gifts of the Holy Spirit** (CGHS)
St Agnes Mission and Orphanage, Gokwe, ZIMBABWE

♀ **Community of the Holy Name** (CHN)
Convent of the Holy Name, P/B 806, Melmoth, Zululand, SOUTH AFRICA
    Convent of the Holy Name, Box 43, Leribe 300, LESOTHO
    CHN Mission House, PO Box 87, Maseru 100, LESOTHO
    St Stephen's Mission, Mohale's Hoek, SOUTH AFRICA
    St Vincent's Mission, P/B 675, Nqutu 3135, Natal, SOUTH AFRICA
    St Luke's Mission, PO Box 175, 3950 Nongoma, SOUTH AFRICA
    St Cyprian's Parish, Box 216, Nkandla, Kwa Zulu, SOUTH AFRICA
    Usuthu Mission, PO Luyengo, SWAZILAND

♀ ♂ **Community of the Holy Transfiguration** (CHT)
St David's Secondary School, P Bag T7904, Bonda Mission, Mutare, ZIMBABWE

♀ **Community of the Resurrection of Our Lord** (CR)
PO Box 72, Grahamstown 6140, SOUTH AFRICA

♀ **Community of St John the Baptist** (CSJB)
PO Box 6, St Cuthbert's, Transkei, SOUTH AFRICA

♀ **Chama cha Maria Mtakatifu** *Community of St Mary of Nazareth and Calvary*
(CMM)
The Convent, Kilimani, SLP 502, Masasi, TANZANIA
  PO Box 116, Newala, Mtwara Region, TANZANIA
  PO Box 162, Mtwara, TANZANIA
  PO Box 45, Tanga, TANZANIA
  PO Box 195, Korogwe, Tanga Region, TANZANIA
  The Convent, PO Kwa Mkono, Handeni, Tanga Region, TANZANIA
  Ilala, PO Box 25016, Dar es Salaam, TANZANIA
  PO Box 150, Njombe, TANZANIA
  PO Box 6, Liuli, Mbinga-Ruvuma Region, TANZANIA
  Sayuni Msima, PO Box 150, Njombe, TANZANIA
  Ndola Convent, PO Box 70172, Ndola, ZAMBIA

♀ **Community of St Michael & All Angels**   **(CSMAA)**
PO Box 79, Bloomfontein 9300, SOUTH AFRICA

♂ **Order of the Holy Cross**   **(OHC)**
Philip Quaque Monastery, PO Box A200, Adisadel, Cape Coast, GHANA
Tel: +233 42 33 671

♀ **Society of the Precious Blood**   **(SPB)**
Priory of Our Lady of Mercy, PO Box 7192, Maseru 100, LESOTHO

♀ **Society of St John the Divine**   **(SSJD)**
St John's House, 43 Florida Road, Greyville, Durban 4001, SOUTH AFRICA

ASIA

♂ **Brotherhood of the Ascended Christ**   **(BAC)**
The Brotherhood House, 7 Court Lane, Delhi 110054, INDIA

♂ **Brotherhood of the Epiphany**   **(BE)**
Oxford Mission, Barisha, Calcutta 700008, INDIA
    Oxford Mission, Bogra Road, PO Box 21, Barisal 8200, BANGLADESH

♀ **Community of Nazareth**   **(CN)**
4-2230 Murey Mitaka Shi, Tokyo 181, JAPAN

♂ **Korean Franciscan Brotherhood**   **(KFB)**
17-3 Chon Dong, Chung Gu, Inchon 400-190, KOREA

AUSTRALASIA & PACIFIC ISLANDS

♀ **The Clare Community** (CC)
Monastery of the BVM, Bucketts Way, Stroud, NSW 2425, AUSTRALIA
Tel: +61 2 4994 5303; Fax: +61 2 4994 5404

♀ **Community of Christ the King** (CCK)
Nason Lodge, Taminick Gap Road, Wangaratta South, VIC 3678, AUSTRALIA
Tel: +61 3 5725 7343

♀ **Community of the Holy Name** (CHN)
The Community House, 40 Cavanagh St, Cheltenham, VIC 3192, AUSTRALIA
Tel: +61 9583 2087; Fax: +61 3 9585 2932

       5 Emerald Street, South Oakleigh, VIC 3167, AUSTRALIA
       Tel: +61 3 9579 2327

. ♀ **Community of the Sacred Name** (CSN)
181 Barbadoes Street, Christchurch 1, NEW ZEALAND *Tel: +64 3 366 8245*
40 Rintoul Street, Newton, Wellington, NEW ZEALAND *Tel: +64 4 389 4580*
St Christopher's Home, PO Box 8232, Nakasi, Suva, FIJI *Tel: +679 47 458*

♂ **Little Brothers of St Francis** (LBF)
'Eremophila', PO Box 162, Tabulam, NSW 2469, AUSTRALIA

♂ **The Melanesian Brotherhood** (MBH)
Headquarters: Tabalia, PO Box 1479, Honiara, Guadalcanal, SOLOMON ISLANDS

♀ **The Melanesian Sisterhood** (MSH)
Headquarters: Mobile Post Bag 7, Verana'aso, Guadalcanal, SOLOMON ISLANDS

♀ **Sisters of the Incarnation** (SI)
House of the Incarnation, 2 Prelate Court, Wynn Vale, SA 5127, AUSTRALIA
Tel: +61 8 8289 3737

♀ **Society of the Sacred Advent** (SSA)
Community House, Lapraik St, Albion, Qld 4010, AUSTRALIA
Tel: +61 7 3262 5511; Fax: +61 7 3862 3296

EUROPE outside the UK

♀ **Community of the Glorious Ascension** (CGA)
Prasada, Quartier Subrane, Montauroux, 83440 Fayenne, Var, FRANCE

♀ **Community of St John the Evangelist** (CSJE)
St Mary's Home, Pembroke Park, Ballsbridge, Dublin 4, EIRE

NORTH AMERICA & the CARIBBEAN

Access to further information about communities in North America can be found on the World Wide Web at http://www.wthree.com/corl/

♀ All Saints Sisters of the Poor   (ASSP)
All Saints' Convent, PO Box 3127, Catonsville, MD 21228, USA
Tel: +1 410 747 4104

St Anna's Home, 2016 Race Street, Philadelphia, PA 19103-1109, USA

♀ Community of the Holy Spirit   (CHS)
St Hilda's House, 621 West 113th Street, New York, NY 10025-7916, USA
Tel: +1 212 666 8249
E-Mail: chs@interport.net

The Melrose Convent, Federal Hill Road, Brewster, NY 10509-9813, USA
Tel: +1 914 278 4854

♀ Community of St Mary *(Eastern Province)*   (CSM)
St Mary's Convent, John Street, Peekskill, New York, NY 10566, USA
Tel: +1 914 737 0113
Fax: +1 914 737 4019
E-Mail: compunun@aol.com

♀ Community of St Mary *(Southern Province)*   (CSM)
St Mary's Convent, 1100 St Mary's Lane, Sewannee, TN 37375 2614, USA
Tel & Fax: +1 615 598 0059

St Mary's Convent, 2619 Sagada, Mount Province, PHILIPPINES

St Mary's Convent, 5608 Monte Vista St, Los Angeles, CA 90042, USA
Tel: +1 213 256 5337

♀ Community of St Mary *(Western Province)*   (CSM)
Mary's Margin, S83 W27815, Beaver Terrace, Mukwonago, WI 53149, USA
Tel & Fax: +1 414 363 8489

♀ Community of the Transfiguration   (CT)
495 Albion Avenue, Cincinnati, OH 45246, USA
Tel: +1 513 771 5291
Fax: +1 513 771 0839

St Mary's Memorial House, 469 Albion Ave, Cincinnati, OH 45246 USA
Tel: +1 513 771 2171

Bethany School, 495 Albion Avenue, Cincinnati, OH 45246, USA
Tel: +1 513 771 7462

PO Box 116, 544-4th Street, Ferndale, CA 95536, USA
Tel: +1 707 786 4117

St Monica's Centre, 10022 Chester Rd, Lincoln Heights, OH 45215, USA
Tel: +1 513 771 7806

San Pedro de Macoris, REPUBLICA DOMINICANA
mailing address: c/o Lynx Air International, DR-STO Box 407052,
Fort Lauderdale, FL 33340, USA

♂ **Order of the Holy Cross** (OHC)
Mount Calvary, PO Box 1296,Santa Barbara, CA 93102, USA
Tel & Fax: +1 805 963 8175

Holy Cross Monastery, PO Box 99, West Park, NY 12493-0099, USA
Tel: +1 914 384 6660
E-Mail: holycross@idsi.net

Incarnation Priory, 1601 Oxford Street, Berkeley, CA 94709, USA
Tel & Fax: +1 510 548 3406

Holy Cross Priory, 204 High Park Avenue, Toronto, Ontario M6P 2S6,
CANADA   *Tel: +1 416 767 9081*
Fax: +1 446 767 4692

♀ ♂ **Order of Julian of Norwich** (OJN)
S10 W26392 Summit Avenue, Waukesha, WI 53188-2636, USA
Tel: +1 414 549 0452
Fax: +1 414 549 0670
E-Mail: ordjulian@aol.com

♀ **Order of St Anne** (OSA)
Convent of St Anne, 1125 North La Salle Street, Chicago, IL 60610, USA
Tel: +1 312 642 3638

♀ **Order of St Anne at Bethany Convent** (OSA)
25 Hillside Avenue, Arlington, MA 02174-0022, USA
Tel: +1 617 643 0921

♂ **Order of St Benedict** (OSB)
St Gregory's Abbey, 56500 Abbey Road,Three Rivers, MI 490930-9595, USA
Tel: +1 616 244 5893
Fax: +1 616 244 8712

♂ **Order of St Benedict** (OSB)
Servants of Christ Priory, 28 West Pasadena Avenue, Phoenix, AZ 85013, USA
Tel: +1 602 248 9321

♀ **Order of St Helena**   **(OSH)**
PO Box 426, Vails Gate, NY 12584, USA
Tel: +1 914 562 0592
Fax: +1 914 562 7051

Convent of St Helena, 134 East 28th St, New York, NY 10016, USA
Tel: +1 212 8890 1124

Convent of St Helena, 1114-21st Avenue, Seattle, WA 98112, USA
Tel: +1 206 325 2830

Convent of St Helena, PO Box 5645, Augusta, GA 30906, USA
Tel: +1 404 798 5201

♀ **Order of the Teachers of the Children of God**   **(TCG)**
5870 East 14th Street, Tucson, AZ 85711, USA
Tel: +1 602 747 5280
Fax: +1 602 747 5236
E-Mail: smltcg@aol.com

Tuller School, Tuller Road, Fairfield, CT 06430, USA
Tel: +1 203 374 3636

Tuller School at Maycroft, PO Box 1991, Sag Harbour, NY 11963, USA
Tel: +1 516 725 1121

♀ **Sisterhood of the Holy Nativity**   **(SHN)**
Convent of the Holy Nativity, 101 East Division St, Fond du Lac, WI 54935, USA
Tel: +1 414 921 2560
E-Mail: shn@ubc.com

St Mary's Retreat House, 505 East Los Olivos St, Santa Barbara,
CA 93105, USA   *Tel: +1 805 682 4117*

♀ **Sisterhood of St John the Divine**   **(SSJD)**
St John's Convent, 1 Botham Road,Willowdale, Ontario M2N 2J5, CANADA
Tel: +1 416 226 2201
Fax: +1 416 222 4442
E-Mail: SSJD.convent@ecunet.org

St John's Rehabilitation Hospital, 285 Cummer Avenue, Willowdale,
Ontario M2M 2G1, CANADA
Tel: +1 416 226 6780
E-Mail: SSJD.hospital@ecunet.org

St John's Priory, 11717 93rd St, Edmonton, Alberta T5G 1E2, CANADA
Tel: +1 403 477 6381
E-Mail: SSJD.priory@ecunet.org

♂ **Society of St John the Evangelist** (SSJE)
980 Memorial Drive, Cambridge, MA 02138, USA
Tel: +1 617 876 3037
Fax: +1 617 876 5210

Cowley Publications, 28 Temple Place, Boston, MA 02111, USA
Bookstore Tel: +1 617 423 4719
Publications Tel: +1 617 728 4450

Emery House, Emery Lane, West Newbury, MA 01985, USA
Tel: +1 508 462 7920
Fax: +1 508 462 0285

♀ **Society of St Margaret** (SSM)
St Margaret's Convent, 17 Highlands Park Street, Roxbury, MA 02119, USA
Tel: +1 617 445 8961

St Margaret's House, 5419 Germantown Ave, Philadelphia, PA 19144-2223, USA   *Tel: +1 215 844 9410*

St Margaret's House, Jordan Road, New Hartford, NY 13413-2395, USA
Tel: +1 617 724 2324

Neale House, 50 Fulton Street, New York, NY 10038-01800, USA
Tel: +1 212 619 2672

St Margaret's Convent, Port-au-Prince, HAITI
mailing address: St Margaret's Convent, P-a-P, c/o Agape Flights Inc.,
7990 15th Street East, Sarasota, FL 34243, USA

♂ **Society of St Paul** (SSP)
PO Box 14350, Palm Desert, CA 92255-4350, USA
Tel: +1 760 568 2200
Fax: +1 760 568 2525

Articles

Retreat - or Advance

by Sister Catherine OHP

Sister Catherine OHP, of St Hilda's Priory in Whitby, on the north Yorkshire coast, reflects on what Anglican Religious Communities offer the increasing number of guests who visit them. She draws from her own experience as guest sister at St Hilda's to consider why hospitality has become such a significant ministry for many communities.

The present Archbishop of Canterbury is quoted as saying that Religious Communities are 'the Church of England's best-kept secret'. On hearing this, one of my young Sisters exclaimed: "but I don't want it to be a secret! I want people to know about us!" It remains true, however, that most people, whether inside or outside church circles, are unaware of the existence of Religious – monks, nuns, friars, brothers and sisters – in the Church of England and assume when they meet us that we must be Roman Catholics. That is understandable perhaps, but incorrect. In fact, there are more than forty Anglican Religious Communities in the UK, spread out in over a hundred and twenty houses throughout the country, with a larger number in the world-wide Anglican Communion. And, many people do know about them, visit them and draw on their resources.

What brings people in ever-increasing numbers to visit a Religious house, join in the community's life, meet and talk to individual brothers or sisters? What can they offer? The leader of one community wrote in a recent letter: "There seems at the moment to be a never-ending stream of demand . . . and an ever-widening interpretation of the magic word *Retreat!*"

This is a comment which would be readily endorsed by others, like myself, who have been given the rôle of guest sister or brother in their community houses. People write, or more often 'phone, at short notice, asking if it is possible to come and stay for a few days. *Away From It All* (Lutterworth Press, Ed. Geoffrey Gerard, 1992, £7.99), the title of a much-consulted guide to retreat houses, expresses the need and the expectation – not that all Religious houses are set in remote places, with spacious grounds and magnificent scenery, although many are. Recently, I recommended a young priest, who was moving from the North, to contact a community house in London's inner city, knowing that, though the externals might be very different from what he had experienced here at Whitby, the essential spirit would be the same – the stepping aside and being welcomed into a life, an 'alternative life-style', with its own distinctive rhythm and coherence.

There is nothing new about such monastic hospitality. The Reception of Guests in *The Rule of St Benedict*, Chapter 53, expresses the basic ideal:

> 'All guests who present themselves are to be welcomed as Christ, who said: "I was a stranger and you welcomed me." Proper honour must be shown to all . . . the prior or abbot and the community are to meet them with all the courtesy of love . . . Christ is to be adored and welcomed in them.'

Yet for many Anglican communities, it is only in the recent past that a ministry of hospitality has assumed a major importance in their lives. As traditional works, such as nursing, teaching, caring for orphans, for the agèd, for vagrants, have in some cases been relinquished, as buildings have become available, and – most important of all – as members of the community have been free and ready to respond to the growing demand for guidance and spiritual friendship, so there has been a marked increase in their provision of 'a place apart' (another guidebook title) to which individuals and groups can come for times of withdrawal and nurture in prayer.

In the case of the Order to which I belong, it was not until major revision of our documents – symptomatic of changes in our community life – took place in the 1960s to produce a new Rule, that a section on hospitality, echoing the Benedictine principles, was included. It begins:

'It has always been a tradition of Religious houses to welcome guests. This is a way in which we show love for our fellow men, and we ourselves are enriched by their presence. Our hope is that all who share our life may find God amongst us, and be renewed in body, mind and spirit.'

In 1971, we completed a new refectory – light, spacious, airy – and this coincided with a new openness to guests, who began to come in greater numbers to share our life in the Priory. Allowing guests into meals, albeit mostly in silence, seemed a great step forward. Then in 1982, a major development in our ministry of hospitality was made possible through the bequest by a local benefactress of a small property set in idyllic surroundings a few miles up the Esk Valley. This became St Oswald's Pastoral Centre, staffed by members of the Order and drawing people from a wide area all the year round for retreats, both individual and corporate.

Like other Religious houses which arrange a programme of bookings, St Oswald's publicises its events in *Retreats* (formerly *Vision*) the annual publication of the National Retreat Movement, itself an eloquent testimony to the extent of the demand and the provision to meet it. Many houses, like our mother house here in Whitby, do not advertise a programme or describe themselves as retreat houses: they stand in their own right, offering to God their life of prayer and work, into which guests are permitted to enter with whatever degree of participation the community has agreed is appropriate and helpful to both themselves and guests. A house so swamped by visitors that the family breaks down is no help to anybody, and that is true of any home. "It's so peaceful here" is the frequently-repeated comment of visitors, but the peace has to be made, and maintained: 'Seek peace and pursue it.' (Ps 34:14)

Nevertheless, a few days living alongside a Religious Community can be a good demythologising exercise for the over-devout, as well as a reassurance for the tentative beginner. Religious tend to be down-to-earth people with a sense of humour. Any tendency towards high-minded piety having been deflated in the realities of the common life, they will show an interest in the mundane creature comforts of life that may surprise visitors who expect a more spiritual emphasis. Instead of finding an insistence on a rigorous asceticism, the guest may be asked more basic questions: 'Are you warm enough? . . . Are you getting enough to eat? Is your bed comfortable?' and the encouragement not to get up early for Morning Prayer – the guest having already apologised for not doing so! Such concern is expressive of a recognition that the whole person – body, mind and spirit – is involved in seeking to advance in one's relationship with God. A retreat is not a holiday – though one definition of retreat is 'holy holiday' – and there has to be some structure, so that this opportunity for disengagement may be a time of attending to God. But neither is it a time for self-flagellation. For many people coming from an over-busy existence, it is hard enough discipline to stop work, drop everything, enter into silence and allow oneself to be 'off the hook'.

Those who make it a regular practice to go on retreat know what they are coming for, and usually need little or no help to get on with it. Others, coming for the first time, may have very specific needs in mind, decisions to make for which they are seeking guidance.

"I've been thinking for some time about the possibility of ordination."

"I recently broke off my engagement."

"My father, whom I've looked after for years, has just died."

"I've got to decide soon whether or not I'm going to change my job."

Those coming with such personal problems and questions need most of all to be helped to listen, not primarily to suggestions and advice that may be offered by the brother or sister who is at hand to help, but to what God is saying in this time of 'elected silence'. My usual advice, for what it is worth, is based on my own experience of being told years ago:

"Don't go into a retreat demanding a blueprint, telling God what you want God to do. Just let go, and allow the Holy Spirit to work in the depths of your heart, through the environment, the silence, through the worship in which you'll participate and the words of Scripture you are exposed to."

And over and over again, I have found that the retreatant will say to me on his or her last evening something like:

"That lesson at Vespers, it just hit the nail on the head . . .

it was amazing ... as if it were directed at me."

"It's uncanny, the Psalms have just kept on emphasizing that one point."

"I've never felt like this before, but this morning at Communion, I really knew

Jesus was giving himself to me and it's going to be alright."

It is when we give our attention, selflessly, to worship God that God can get through to us and lead us on.

Some who come on a first visit may have been advised to 'get yourself a spiritual director', a term which many of us would eschew, preferring words like companion, fellow-pilgrim, listener, friend. In practice, the need (which I share) is less for an expert on prayer (who would dare claim to be that?) than for a confidant, someone to whom I can pour out problems and concerns, who will monitor the disciplines of prayer undertaken (or not begun to think about?) and help to discern how life is shaping up as a whole. This, I have found, is very true of those who ask to come to learn more about prayer. The story may begin with how difficult the speaker finds it to pray, but very quickly moves into statements about his or her spouse, neighbours, vicar, colleagues, all contributing to the problem! And so it is necessary to emphasize that prayer cannot be seen in isolation, that life is a whole, and that 'spiritual life' is not in a separate compartment.

So what do they find, these retreatants? What is on offer in Religious houses? First of all, there is *space:* permission to do nothing, to disengage, relax, sleep; time to 'stand and stare'; to enjoy a leisurely meal, bath and book; a space perhaps enhanced by the adjuncts of gardens (that they don't have to tend), scenery, good walks. Time to let the soul catch up with the body. Such is the hoped-for provision of any retreat house.

Then, *quiet*: the rare opportunity to experience a *silence* which is more than the absence of noise, but rather a positive component in the daily pattern to which corporate consent has been given, thus providing the space within which inner quiet may be experienced. In a noisy world, this provision, built on the common observance of times and places of silence, may be the most distinctive gift that a Religious Community can offer to retreatants.

Prayer and *worship*: a stream into which one may enter and on which one may be borne along; the daily rhythm of communal offering imparting a sense of belonging. The worship does not depend on guests for its continuation – that is a relief to both weary clergy and disheartened or apprehensive laity. It goes on as the work of the community, however depleted their numbers are. And it is this sense of corporate endeavour, of shared purpose, of *community*, that (ideally) produces the atmosphere of peace which those coming in from outside can sense, even when those inside feel anything but peaceful. There is *structure*, not imposed for regimentation, but provided as the support for freedom to allow the spirit to breathe.

From all this, it will, I hope, be apparent that the members of Religious Communities, far from considering themselves as an élite body of spiritual gurus, are most conscious, quite simply, of their corporate life as the chief thing they have to offer to those seeking God. Opinions differ as to the need for specialist training in spiritual direction. Many Religious have undergone such training and use it both in conducting retreats and in guiding individuals. But, I believe, all would agree that it is primarily through our faithfulness to the life of prayer and the tradition of our community that we are equipped to help others go forward on their way.

Chapel of Saint Hilda's Priory, Whitby

Important Advice
about Going on Retreat
by the Editors

Many of the communities in this directory have accommodation for people who wish to go on retreat. To help you, here are a few important points to note before you plan your visit.

ABOUT BOOKING
1. Always write to the community and make a booking for your stay. Do not turn up unannounced. Many communities' guest accommodation is fully booked in advance and you need to arrange your visit in good time with the guest brother or sister.

2. If you have to cancel your visit, please inform the community as soon as possible. This will enable another retreatant to use the room. If you book a long time in advance, please confirm the booking by telephone a few weeks beforehand.

3. When you book, tell the guest brother or sister if you have particular dietary needs, for example, if you are vegetarian. Also make known any other needs you may have, perhaps concerned with any disability, such as that you require a ground floor room. It is frustrating for everyone if you only make these requirements known once you are in residence.

4. Before you go, make sure you have with you all your essential personal items, such as a tooth-brush. Check too if you need to take your own towel and soap; this varies from community to community.

ABOUT STAYING
5. Respect the traditions of the house, for example, keep the silences as requested. Remember that some other guests may be on silent retreats, even if you are not, and they will not wish to engage in conversation. In many Religious houses, some, if not all, meals are taken in silence.

6. Remember that convents and monasteries and friaries are the homes of Religious brothers and sisters. Only use the parts of the house which are available to guests and treat the facilities with the care you would use in your own home.

7. In chapel, be thoughtful in participating at the Office and other services. Follow the lead of the community and join in with discretion. Even if you think your way would be an improvement, do not try to take over the recitation of psalms or the singing of hymns.

8. Most Religious houses give a guide as to the cost of your stay. Be honest and give what you can afford. If you are able to give more than the basic cost, this is of help to the community in caring for those less fortunate. Most communities are charities and depend on your generosity.

Religious in General Synod

by Father Aidan Mayoss CR

In the 1997, Church House issued a report from a review group which suggested General Synod should be smaller in size. The recommendations included Religious Communities' representation being reduced from five to three members, and if accepted, this would be implemented with effect from 2005. At at time too when many urge Religious to 'work on the margins' of society, **Father Aidan Mayoss CR** *(one of the serving General Synod representatives for Religious) reflects on the presence of Religious at the heart of the Church's government.*

At the thought of Religious being in the General Synod in particular, and the corridors of power in general, many, both within and without the Religious Life, think (if they do not actually utter) the words of Psalm 131:

'Lord, I am not high-minded, I have no proud looks.

I do not exercise myself in great matters, in things that are too high for me.'

In 1919, when the Enabling Act set up the Church Assembly, and thus for the first time brought the laity into the governance of the Church of England, there was no specific place allotted to lay Religious, their only way forward would be to take pot luck through the diocesan system. As far as I am aware none did. For the clergy, provided that you were licensed by a bishop, you could stand and vote in the elections for Convocations. A few did. With the setting up of the General Synod in 1970, provision was made for Religious to form one of several special constituencies and elect their own representatives, one clerical and one lay for the Northern

(from left to right) **Sister Teresa CSA, Brother Tristam SSF, Father Aidan Mayoss CR, Sister Hilary CSMV, Sister Margaret Shirley OHP**

province and the same for the south. Later, a second lay representative was added for the Southern province, making a total of five. Even under new proposals, aimed at reducing total numbers on Synod, Religious remain almost the sole special constituency, and would be given three representatives (one clerical, two lay). So we are there by right. The Church still wants us there, as a constituent representing an often hidden part of itself.

In the 1940s and 1950s, men like Gregory Dix OSB and Raymond Raynes CR were the leaders of the catholic wing of the Church, not just organising opposition to the church unity scheme in South India, but providing balanced, considered and frequently witty speeches, which were listened to, admired and often acted upon. For both of these men, debate was something at which they excelled. The time was also ripe. Things are different now and the debating chamber is but a small part of the work done by many members of Synod. We come together twice a year: for the inside of a week at Westminster and four days over a weekend at York.

On these occasions we are on display and a lot of work is done. All have their parts to play, and there are occasional contributions from Religious in the debating chamber. We are not given to the common synodical fault of 'not being heard for their much speaking', but, because of our different perspective, at times we are able to illuminate what is before the house, quite apart from any special expertise one or another of us might have. Mission, liturgy, spirituality, theological education and ecumenism are more to our taste than pensions, churchwardens, or some of the other matters on the Synod agenda.

This is the 'up-front' bit, and, popularly I suppose, a bit like the House of Commons; influence and significance are judged by the amount of times one has been successful in catching the chair's eye, inventing amendments which will ensure that one speaks, or asking difficult questions of those in authority. This is not, however, the main work.

The committees of the General Synod are a key to its work. Even under the Turnbull Report's proposals for change, there will still be committees and working parties on which Synod members are expected to serve. Synod members are elected to these committees by their fellow members in elections which are keenly contested. As representatives of Synod, those elected are committed to a heavy workload, co-operating with the staff who run the Church's departments and they have the responsibility for the right use of the Church's resources of people and money, as well as sometimes initiating new responses to different situations. It is in this sort of work, as well as the informal connections that result in living alongside one another for the four days (at York especially) that brains are picked, experience drawn out and friendships developed across what, in another place, would be called 'party lines'.

Time was when the Religious in the Church Assembly led the Catholic wing; now we belong to more than one of the several 'parties' and groupings: Catholic, Affirming Catholic, Open Synod, Open Evangelical and the more conservative Evangelical group, and no doubt more. There is help and strength to be gained from membership of these groups, but it is rare, if at all, that they vote to a man or a woman the same way, according to the party line. Ideally, we should never have to vote at all in a Christian assembly, but it does help, in some matters at least, to have a clear indication of the mind of Synod, and it is necessary if this is a matter which has to go on to be laid before Parliament before changing the teaching of the Church, its authorised services, or the way in which we do things. It is significant that sometimes the vote belies the voices from the floor, whose shrillness is discovered to belong to no more than a tiny minority.

I think two basic questions still remain. Why should there be Religious in the Synod at all? Is it right that we should be involved in this sort of decision-making?

Those who drew up membership of Synod and those who approve it, obviously thought, and still think, that Religious should have a place. We are not part of the day-to-day structures of parish, deanery and diocese, so we cannot be threatened by the 'system', nor can we be promoted through it. We have no need to be 'noticed' – although I have had my summer habit, worn at York in the usual heat wave, described as 'power dressing'. It is very difficult to describe the gifts that we have from our different – but certainly not better – commitment to the Christian life and to the Church. We are also the representatives of Religious and can make the concerns and requests of our electorate known. After a while we learn our way around and whom to ask about what, which is much more effective than making a great fuss or putting someone 'on the spot'. Some of us have a particular interest or skill and it is right this should be used for the Church at large. Whilst this could be done by co-option, it is far better that Synod has an elected member around in the corridors (or, at York, lakeside and bars). These corridors are not ones of 'power' but of responsibility, interest and friendship, and where a great deal of Synod work is done.

But the question still remains: should we be there at all? One remembers Lord Acton's phrase that power corrupts. So is Synod membership corrupting? Well, it certainly can be. For some members, Synod seems to loom larger in their lives than it ought. Here I am not writing about the wholly admirable staff, but members who seem ever to be thinking up questions, seeking the eye of the chair, and writing to members in between sessions (this is sometimes with first-class postage and 26p x 570 is £148.20). Maybe the proposed new electoral system, when passed, will remove some if not all of them. We Religious, who live according to the rule of our communities and orders, are not free agents to do as we please. Time occupied by Synod and committees, groups and working parties, has to be balanced by the other things that we are called upon to do, nor must it erode our commitment to the immediate worship and service of God. If it does that then it is we, not the Synod, that have got things wrong. It does and should take up time, and some things that once I did I can no longer do, but I would hate to feel that Synod is taking all my time and strength and energy. For if it were, I don't think I would be right to stay in it. A balance has to be struck and maintained.

I was elected to the Advisory Board of Ministry and within that Board I serve on a sub-committee to do with pre-theological education. Not only does the Community of the Resurrection have a long history of theological education, it has run a pre-theological education scheme. In my other work in parishes and retreats and spiritual direction, I come across people who might develop a vocation to ministry and those already ordained who share with me the joys and difficulties of their experience. So the time spent on reading Synod reports, and helping to form a mind on the matter, has a value for my other work.

My experience of Synod is that the Religious are valued by those who understand what we are about – although, alas, there are many who don't, as yet, know all that much. But we are used. Our perspective is different from the experience of the vowed life. In some ways we have a duty to be the 'gadfly on the body politic', possibly to have a prophetic rôle warning Synod. Being on General Synod also means that one is on the Diocesan Synod and the Deanery Synod too. Wearisome and irrelevant as these bodies often are, the presence of Religious is valued there too and we need to be seen as part of the Church. If we, as we surely should, long for an increase in vocations, the Synods are one place where we are on display in a very non-upfront way.

Synod membership is a responsibility which is placed upon us by our fellow Religious. Under the proposed changes, with fewer representatives, I hope that we shall have more elections. For it is no use moaning about the way the Church is going if once every five years, at the time of the elections, brothers and sisters have to have their arms twisted to stand. I firmly believe that we ought to be there, despite the fact that at times it can be harassing and lonely. Synod members who are Religious are not trespassing in the corridors of power, but representatives of a part of the living Church, who both deserve and need lots of prayers.

Keith Ellis, with permission

The General Synod of the Church of England, meeting at Westminster

At the name of Jesus, every knee shall bow
and every tongue confess, 'Jesus Christ is Lord', to the glory of God the Father.
Philippians 2. 11

Priesthood in a Women's Community

by Sister Helen Loder SSM

It is now five years since the Church of England's General Synod voted to allow women to be ordained as priests. In this article, a sister of the Society of St Margaret, from St Saviour's Priory, Haggerston, reflects on the impact her own priesting has had within her community. **Sister Helen SSM was professed in 1970 and was ordained priest in 1995.**

Any reflection on priesthood in a women's community is bound to be determined by certain factors: the brevity of the actual experience of such priesthood, the percentage of acceptance of women's ministry within a community, and the style of leadership already in place. The context of this reflection is a community in which one sister has been ordained priest for a mere two years, where the acceptance of such ministry has been unanimous (although it is important to note that the community is an autonomous house of a larger Society in which the two integrities are represented), and where the structure of authority has undergone a radical change in the last six years.

Priesthood in community presents the Church with a very real opportunity to explore its prophetic rôle. In the first place, God's call to such priesthood comes from within the community it seeks to serve, with the Chapter's consent and approval. The response to such a call, and responsibility for it, is therefore not carried by the individual alone, but by all its members. In this way, priestly ministry, from the start, becomes just one part of the recognition of the ministry of each, and part of the mutuality of respect and care for all

Sister Monica serving Sister Helen, also serving!

within the community, rather than a vocation and rôle set apart from the rest. The result of such an experience has been not the down-grading of priestly ministry, but a new recognition of the value and validity of the part played by each sister within her community from the housekeeper to the gardener to one who cleans the toilets.

Priesthood has often in the past been equated with leadership and the exercise of power. Our community, however, has already moved from a hierarchical structure to exploring a style of leadership which, while it brings direction and unity to the group, also exists to facilitate the community's ability to discern its charism and contemporary implications for itself (Joan Chittister, *The Fire in these Ashes*, Sheed & Ward, Kansas City, 1995, p 131). In this context, there need be no tension between the leadership of the community and the authority given at ordination: both co-exist as part of the same valuing and affirmation of the responsibility of each member to discern the will of God. The opportunity of exercising priesthood without leadership has a prophetic quality, particularly important to the Church today as it seeks to re-evaluate the nature of ordination. As Penny Jamieson, Bishop of Dunedin in New Zealand, comments on the contribution by women in non-stipendiary ministry:

'They seek to be priests within and for their communities, but not necessarily to equate their priesthood with leadership.

I have a strong feeling here that, in the ministry these women are offering, God is doing a new thing, the dimensions of which we cannot yet see.'

(Penny Jamieson, *Living at the Edge*, Mowbray, London, 1997, p 50)

Perhaps the most radical change that priesthood in community brings (and perhaps the most alarming to some members of the episcopate) is its sacramental autonomy. A women's community with its own priesthood is no longer dependent on the priestly ministry from outside. This has had two major effects: now when priests from outside are invited to celebrate the Eucharist (and we have gratefully retained our rota of local male and female priests who come in five days a week), they know it is no longer from necessity, but because we value their individual ministry. Similarly, Eucharists which we celebrate together with one of our Sisters as priest takes on a new dimension, previously never before experienced in the history of women's communities in England. For just as the call to priesthood and the response to that call has been seen as the responsibility of the whole community, so celebrating the Eucharist is seen not so much as the responsibility of the individual, but something in which, in a new way, each increasingly plays an equal, if different part. The well-known words of Michael Ramsey on a priest's intercessions now take on a new meaning:

'It is like Aaron of old who went into the holy of holies wearing a breastplate with jewels representing the tribes of Israel whose priest he was: he went near to God with the people on his heart.'

(Michael Ramsey, *The Christian Priest Today*, SPCK, London, 1972, p 15)

Our experience today is that each of us is called to approach God corporately at the altar with the people in our hearts, for celebrating the Eucharist together within community provides an opportunity to explore new liturgies, new ways of celebrating our particular vocation and charism, new ways of exercising our ministry within the sacrament.

Another effect of priesthood within the community is that it highlights the fact that it is now possible for women's communities to choose whether or not to have an outside chaplain/warden (a rôle never needed by most men's communities) as the liturgical, and similar, functions which he had been accustomed to perform are gradually taken on from within the community. Thus, in our community, the chaplain's rôle had already for many years become less as Sisters became free to choose their own confessors and spiritual directors, and once the Mother took on the clothing of novices and the reception of vows at Profession, and we became responsible for counting the votes at elections, etc., the chaplain himself proposed that his rôle had become redundant. Now having a Sister celebrating at a Profession Eucharist, giving the last rites and taking a Sister's Funeral Eucharist feels not only appropriate but part of the same development. (There is no plan for hearing confessions within community; it is neither necessary nor desirable and, given our tradition, would border on the incestuous.)

Finally, although priesthood within community, for the first time in our history, places one of our members under direct episcopal authority (her ministry has to be licensed by the local bishop), it is still an opportunity to explore priesthood and community on the edge. Many of us might feel that being a woman already places us at the edge of society; having a woman priest in community gives us a new way of working on the frontiers (where as a member of a Religious Community we are already called to be) amongst the dispossessed, the despised, the forgotten. Moreover, the priest's spirituality becomes one of vulnerability; it is a humbling task to stand up and preside at the Eucharist amongst Sisters who experience only too often one's weaknesses, shortcomings and sins: not much scope for pride or relishing status here. The edge is the frontier, the place of transfiguration, for, as John O'Donohue wrote,

> 'The edge is a precarious place. Here change continually creates new perception. Here ideas stay alert and tentative in their urgency to mirror the new shapes that come across the frontier.' The Way (1995/83)

Celebrating the Eucharist at St Saviour's Priory, Haggerston

JUBILEE 2000
A debt-free start for a billion people

Sister Emma Karran, Novice SSC

*Many of the children born in the poorer countries of the world are inevitably trapped in poverty from the moment of birth. It is a poverty perpetuated by debts which can never be paid off, debts owed by these poorer countries to the West. This burden is therefore being maintained in our name. A campaign called **Jubilee 2000** proposes we celebrate the new millennium by cancelling the unrepayable debts, so offering hope for both creditor and debtor. In this article, Sister Emma, a novice from Tymawr Convent, looks at the Jubilee 2000 campaign and the reasons to support it.*

Many Anglican Religious Communities began as pioneers in social reform. From their beginnings in the nineteenth century, there was a passion for justice, which fired their prayer and work in prisons, hospitals, schools and among the poor in our cities. Today our world, including parts of the UK, still has a desperate need for our prayers and action. Many Anglican communities are praying and working for the Jubilee 2000 proposals, alongside their brothers and sisters in other churches.

So what is Jubilee 2000? It is a campaign whose concern is that billions of people in the world's poorest countries are enslaved by debts, which were caused by governments on their behalf. These debts started as easy credit pushed by rich lenders, but now the poor will never be able to repay them. The debts serve to enrich lenders, but leave children malnourished and their families destitute. Jubilee 2000 is campaigning to celebrate the new millennium by lifting this burden of unrepayable debt from the poorest countries.

Jubilee 2000 describes itself as an educational organisation allied to a campaign. It is not a fund-raising movement. The Jubilee Proposal is:

a one-off cancellation by the year 2000
of the backlog of unrepayable debt
owed by the poorest countries
on a case by case basis.

To achieve this, Jubilee 2000 aims to work at three different levels:
Firstly: to build up a membership of concerned, informed members in the UK and abroad; secondly, to engage in discussion on the debt issue with economists, politicians and decision-makers; thirdly, as the millennium approaches, to use a huge media campaign in 1998-1999 to bring pressure upon world leaders to make the necessary changes. But what can we do?

Be Informed

The debt situation arose in the 1970s, when Western banks needed to lend their large reserves of money to avoid an international financial crisis. Huge sums were lent to Third World countries, whose economies were then doing well, but who needed money to maintain development and meet the rising costs of oil. The debts then spiralled out of control because of two factors. First, interest rates rose massively, so debt repayments increased dramatically. Second, the prices of primary products went down on average by 30% because too many countries, advised by the West, were producing the same crops. Therefore, Third World incomes plunged. The poorest countries in the world were earning less but having to pay much more. In 1982, Mexico told its creditors that it could not repay its debts.

By the 1980s, the World Bank and the International Monetary Fund had become involved in re-scheduling debts and in providing new loans under strict conditions to help pay the interest. The conditions take the form of Structural Adjustment Programmes (SAPs), which tie the governments of debtor countries to very strict economic programmes. The imposed conditions aimed to help a country pay its debts by earning more hard currency, by increasing exports and decreasing imports. However, in all countries applying SAPs, the poor have been hit the hardest, because these programmes usually include:

1. Spending less on health, social services and education, so that only those who can pay have access to them. Africa now spends four times as much on its loans than on health care. Over 500,000 children die each year as a consequence of the cutbacks in health services.

2. Devaluing the national currency, lowering export earnings and increasing import costs.

3. Cutting back on food subsidies, which can sometimes entail the prices of essential goods soaring in a matter of days.

4. Cutting jobs and wages for workers in government industries and services.

5. Encouraging privatisation of public industries, including selling to foreign investors.

6. Taking over subsistence farms growing staple foods to create large-scale export crop farms. Consequently, farmers are left with no land on which to grow their food, and few of them are employed on the large farms.

The debt crisis is clearly a disaster for the people who live in Third World debtor countries. Each year these countries pay the West three times more in debt repayments than they receive in aid. Zambia was once one of the richest countries in Africa. Today, every Zambian citizen owes the country's creditors over £ 565, more than three times the average annual salary. The results of international debt, however, also 'boomerang' back to hurt the rich countries of the First World. In her book *The Debt Boomerang*, Susan George lists six areas in which the debt crisis affects the creditor countries as much as the debtors.

1 KILLING THE ENVIRONMENT

Brazil is one of the largest debtors, owing US$112 billion. It is also the world's largest deforester, cutting a staggering 50,000 square kilometres of forest each year. The forests are chopped down by loggers, developers and farmers, as well as by ordinary people pushed off the land by large development projects.

2 LOST JOBS AND MARKETS

Debt means poor countries can not afford imports. This helps cause global recession and a rise in Western unemployment. It is also cheaper to import Third World goods, which equally has an effect on factory and farm output – and therefore jobs – in the West. One key recommendation of Structural Adjustment Programmes is privatisation. This means multinational companies can set up in poorer countries, where they can pay lower wages and where laws about working hours and conditions are often less strict. The company can therefore make a bigger profit from the Third World, where workers are forced to accept bad working conditions, than maintaining jobs in Western countries.

3 FUELLING THE DRUGS TRADE

Almost all the major drug-producing countries also have high international debts. To repay debts, they need hard currency from the sale of commodities, like cocoa, whose value has been falling. Meanwhile, cocaine prices have been rising, so countries turn to the drugs trade to raise foreign currency and to survive. For example, 40% of Bolivia's work-force depend on the drugs trade for a living.

4 BAILING OUT THE BANKS

The four main High Street banks in the UK – Lloyds, NatWest, Midland and Barclays – have all been involved in lending to the Third World. For these banks, however, the worst of the crisis is over. All of them have sold off large portions of their debt by one means or another. Lloyds, Midland and Barclays have all made substantial profits from selling, exchanging and making provision for Third World debts.

5 IMMIGRATION

There are about 100 million legal and illegal immigrants and refugees today. Most of them are in the countries of the Third World but an increasing number are arriving in the West. The desire to migrate will not change, no matter how many laws are created to prevent immigration, unless conditions in the sending countries improve so that people can make an adequate living and support their families. Reducing the debt burden would enable poorer countries to improve living conditions and so keep their active workforce rather than losing them through immigration.

6 CONFLICT AND WAR

Britain uses export credits to subsidise arms sales to the South. In 1993-4, 50% of all export credits provided by the Department of Trade and Industry (DTI) to exporters were for arms sales. In time, these credits became debts for poorer countries. 96% of the debts owed to Britain by poor countries are owed to the Export Credit Department of the DTI. Debt can also lead and contribute to war. As countries become poorer, one reaction is violence and protest among their people. Escalation of this can end in war. As governments then respond by spending more on armaments, they have even fewer resources left to relieve poverty. So the cycle of war and debt continues.

Sign the Petition

Jubilee 2000 are circulating a petition for signature by millions of people around the world, to become a global plea for a new debt-free start for a billion people. It will be submitted to the leaders of the richest countries, as the world's biggest creditors, at the G7 summit in 1999. Copies of the petition can be obtained from the *Jubilee 2000* office, at the address at the end of this article.

Work to spread the word

Write to your local MP, your MEP and the Managing Director of the IMF (Mr Michel Camdessus, International Monetary Fund, H Street NW, Washington DC 20009, USA) about the Jubilee proposal. Write and ask your bank about their policies on debt. If you are not satisfied with the response, consider depositing your money with *The Co-operative Bank* or *Friends Provident*, both of which are committed to ethical investment and have no involvement with Third World debt.

Consider using fairly-traded products where possible. For example, Café Direct is a fair-traded coffee which gives the farmer more direct benefit. Organisations such as Traidcraft and Oxfam offer an increasing range of such goods. Religious Communities, offering hospitality to many visitors and guests, can play a rôle in witnessing on the debt issue simply through their shopping policies.

Jubilee 2000 has published an excellent book *The Debt Cutter's Handbook*, on which much of this article is based. It contains a fuller description of the background and present realities of the debt crisis, and also ideas for individual action and group discussion. Some pages can be made into posters. The book also includes material for biblical reflection, meditations and prayers, and an excellent article by Roger Forster, looking at a biblical response to the situation. It can be obtained from:

Jubilee 2000, PO Box 100, London SE1 7RT
Tel: 0171 401 9999; Fax: 0171 401 3999; E-Mail: j2000c@gn.apc.org

One of the closest parallels to the debt crisis is the Atlantic slave trade. It too was a system of international oppression accepted for centuries as a normal and necessary part of trade and life. Influential people like William Wilberforce took up the cause, but it needed the agreement and support of thousands of ordinary people to ensure the abolition of the slave trade.

There are people in positions of power in both North and South who are eager to see a fairer world with debts cancelled. However, the support of thousands of people in the North is needed to bring pressure on decision-makers into implementing basic change. It is an opportunity for Christians to work in partnership with others throughout the world. It is an opportunity for Anglican Religious Communities to support such work with prayer and action. It is an opportunity not to be missed, because, in the words of Bishop Rowan Williams, we shall be a 'smaller, shabbier, more unholy people if we are complicit in debt'.

Vocation

Sister Teresa Mary SSB
interviewed by Isabel Losada

*Isabel Losada has interviewed novices in a range of Anglican communities. It is hoped the work will be published as a book. In the interviews, the sisters speak of their histories and hopes and the call to Religious Life. In this edited extract, **Sister Teresa Mary SSB** shares her thoughts on her vocation and prayer. **Sister Teresa** was a novice at the time of the interview in 1996. A year later, she took life vows in the Society of the Sisters of Bethany.*

My friends all thought it was quite natural that I should become a nun. But there was one group of people who seemed totally amazed: that was those who went to my church. You would have expected them to be happy to hear that I was going to dedicate my life to the God that they worship every Sunday. But they were all shocked. I remember one woman saying, 'what do you want to do that for?'

* * *

Teresa Mary SSB

When I first visited the convent I had every intention of hating it. I thought I would see this bunch of miserable elderly nuns with their heads bowed saying the rosary. But people smiled and laughed and spoke to me and I couldn't hate it at all.

* * *

I woke up one morning, and I don't very often dream, but this particular morning I knew what I had dreamt. I don't know if people want to call it a dream or a vision, but I prefer to call it a dream, a powerful dream. In it, I saw myself in a habit. I had never thought at all about joining a Religious Community. I assumed all nuns were Roman Catholic.

I rang my Mum a week later

and told her that I had come to a crossroads in life and didn't know which way to go next. She said, 'I know what you are going to do. You are going to join a convent. You told me when you were about eight years old and I always knew it would happen.' I was amazed. I had no recollection of this. On the strength of this I went to my priest to offer to become a Roman Catholic. He explained that this wasn't necessary and I was given a list of Anglican communities. I tried writing but tore up all my letters. The following day I went to a day of prayer at Guildford Cathedral. While I was waiting for the rest of my parish to arrive, I saw a nun and went bounding after her and said, 'Excuse me, I think I want to be a nun.' And it was Sister Elvina from the Sisters of Bethany. She smiled and said she would meet me at lunchtime and that was how I came here.

The first day I came to the community, I saw the window frames were painted green, just like my grandad's house. The gardens were beautiful and it felt like I'd come home. In most Anglican communities, twenty-five is the minimum age for taking life vows but this community does not have a minimum age of entry. I had my dream in February, met Sister Elvina in April and in October I arrived. I was twenty-three.

* * *

I do not feel the presence of God twenty-four hours a day. However, it is a knowledge that God is there, a knowledge that you can't back up with logic. My prayer life is erratic and I don't always have a wonderful experience every time I pray. But I do have a prayer life. My way of describing prayer is that it is a communication with God. It isn't always a two-way conversation. God is always ready to listen to me. When I pray is the time when I hope I listen. I pray twenty-four hours a day because I'm living for God, living with God. My specific times of meditation are my quality one-to-one times. I aim to think nothing but God. But my concentration is still pretty hopeless and if I hear a noise I will look to see where it has come from.

When I first came here, I had two half-hour sessions of meditation a day and I was lucky if I could keep still for a minute. As for trying to concentrate for a half an hour, it was an absolute impossibility. I now get up earlier than I have to in order to get one hour's prayer in. I'm finding I'm more comfortable with the one-to-one relationship with God. I still get angry with God and I have been known to throw a slipper in the direction of the crucifix when I'm in my room. I use the worst unrepeatable language with God sometimes but if you love someone you feel free to show all your emotions with them. I feel God should intervene more often. Far more often.

I use different forms of prayer. Sometimes I use a mantra, which is a verse or a word that you keep repeating all the time, like alleluia. I also use the Orthodox rosary, the Catholic rosary, but most of the time I just sit. There is a proverb from 5,000 BC that says, 'The way to do is to be.' This is what I'm learning: it is enough just to be there for God. I don't try to do anything or even be anything, and if a thought comes I just let it float away. I'm just being, like a tree is just being. I don't get a wonderful sensation every time – in fact it very rarely happens – but when it does it re-affirms my beliefs. It is difficult to describe one of these special times. It's a bit like lying on a gigantic bean bag and you can make it comfortable in every position you want.

I have never heard a voice. God does not speak to me over a tannoy system. I feel God speaks to me through emotions and feelings. I like to have a good cry. I do get angry but I don't tend to do it in the presence of other people. I usually wait until I can be alone with God. God speaks to me through my gut and through the working out of things.

* * *

There was the usual comment that I was running away from life to go to a convent. Of course, what people don't realize is that when you go to a convent you run slap-bang into yourself. Actually, there was nothing I was running away from. I'd just been offered the job I wanted at the salary I wanted. And I suppose some people thought that I must be thinking 'I'm on the shelf, no-one is going to love me, so I'll join the convent instead.' But that simply wasn't true.

Some people say that I am missing out on the most important experience of life by not marrying and having a sexual relationship. But, at the risk of sounding absurd, I've got God. Some people feel fulfilled in their job. Some people, if they are Christians, feel that going to church once a week and saying their prayers is going to fulfil their life. I don't feel as if I'm missing out. I feel that I'm gaining and giving more than I ever did before. I feel so free to be myself here.

It is important to say that there is no padlock on the door and no wall around the convent. If I did feel differently in my late thirties and wanted to leave, it is the equivalent of a divorce and about as difficult where paperwork and emotional upheaval are concerned, but there is no electric fence.

People say that it is an un-natural life and I totally agree. It is far more normal to get married and have children. But God calls people to all walks of life. Jesus never married. He lived a life of celibacy, obedience to his father God and a life of poverty. He said that he had nowhere to lay his head. Most people are called to the 'Adam and Eve' life, where man is made for woman, and woman is made for man. But I'm very happy in this life.

I can relax and be me here so fully and I can have time with God. Before I came into community, I tried desperately to have a disciplined spiritual life. I didn't. I have very little self-discipline. In one way, if you want to be a Christian and committed to your spirituality, Religious Life is a very easy option. You have a timetable. You have help and discipline. You never have to worry about when and where to pray. I don't have to make sixty outgoing phone calls a day. If I don't finish the work I have to do today, it doesn't matter; I can do it tomorrow. If I get way behind, someone will help me. If you are ill, the sisters look after you. If you have joyous news, it is news they all enjoy. We don't just share possessions, we share our lives. When my natural family go away, they send a card to all of the sisters. Because my sisters have accepted my family so much, my family can accept them.

The sisters don't judge you at all. They don't care if you get spots or get fat. They embrace you. You accept that everyone has funny ways. Not only do we wear habits, but we may have irritating habits as well. But here it doesn't matter. You don't have the worries of fashion, jobs, money or work, so you can free yourself to be with God and pray on behalf of those people that do have worries.

You are free to be with God all the time.

Solitude and Community

by Brother Ramon SSF

An increase in vocations to an eremitical life-style has been a noted feature of Religious Life in the past thirty years. **Brother Ramon SSF** *felt a call to the hermit life even before beginning to test his vocation with the Franciscans in 1976. The year before he had attended the Hermit Symposium, held in Wales, which was a gathering of about thirty men and women interested in this particular call. It included both those who were following an eremitic call and others who were knowledgeable about the history of hermit life, drawn from Orthodox, Anglican and Roman Catholic traditions. One of the main themes of the conference was an exploration of the difficulties of following such a vocation in the West.*

Following two six-month periods of experimentation in solitude, **Brother Ramon** *began a serious exploration of the hermit life in 1990, continued permanently in a hut enclosure in the grounds of Glasshampton monastery, one of the SSF houses. Here, he reflects on his personal call and his relationship with his community.*

Thomas Merton has always been a radical catalyst for my thinking, praying and life-style as a Franciscan. I would like to quote a significant paragraph from his later writing, and indicate how it works for me in the context of my vocation within the Society of St Francis.

Brother Ramon SSF

'The monastic hermit realizes that he owes his solitude to his community and owes it in more ways than one. First of all, the community has bestowed it upon him in an act of love and trust. Second, the community helps him to stay there and make a go of it, by prayers and by material aid. Finally, the hermit 'owes this solitude' to the community in the sense that his solitary life with its depth of prayer and awareness is his contribution to the community, something that he gives back to his 'monastic Church' in return for what he has been given.'

(Thomas Merton, *Contemplation in a World of Action*, Allen & Unwin, London, 1971, p 242)

First, the community has bestowed my solitude on me in an act of love and trust. From the first, I trusted SSF to listen to me as I spoke of the increasing pull toward solitude. I did expect a certain amount of misunderstanding, though, and even opposition. But the fact is that although there was one gentle but real confrontation about my reluctance to become a member of our SSF Chapter, I have only experienced 'love and trust' over the whole period.

I have felt loved, appreciated and encouraged by the community, and because SSF has trusted me to live, act and respond in terms of the Gospel and our covenanted vows, I have endeavoured to return that trust. Misunderstanding and opposition has not been evident. I have not acted at any point without prior consultation and sharing, and there has been a warm and reciprocal awareness that I had the freedom to develop in my own way and not according to some preconceived or traditional mould. Of course we both kept before us the great tradition of contemplative life within the Church catholic.

My threefold inspiration has been: a) my own Celtic roots; b) the desert father tradition; c) the vision and lifestyle of St Francis and the early days of the Order. The freedom to experiment with this marvellous 'threefold cord' makes me immensely grateful to SSF, and we have been able to affirm that it is not simply 'my vocation' but 'our vocation'. This has been brought about particularly because of the 'three wise men' who support me. They are: Dr Donald (A.M.) Allchin, my spiritual director; Brother Anselm SSF, who was Minister Provincial when I went off experimenting with solitude in 1982 and 1984 and initiated me into the real thing in 1990; and Brother Damian SSF, who is our present Minister Provincial. This 'act of love and trust' expresses a relationship between us and the SSF Chapter, and is not primarily a bureaucratic decision or transaction. I must add that during the decade before her death in 1988, Mother Mary Clare SLG was my spiritual director, and especially after the Hermit Symposium in 1975 at St David's, she enabled me to retain balance and humour, seeing things in perspective during the time of experimentation.

Second, the community helps me to stay there and make a go of it, by prayers and by material aid. Certainly, I had sufficient trust and determination to go off into the desert. Because of the powerful initiatory push which came as a result of the Hermit Symposium, I would have attempted it anyway – even as a parish priest and without the support of a monastic community. But I may well have made a mess of it, or suffered because of my own idiosyncratic nature. I need my community to support, encourage and enliven me in my vocation.

The fact is that I have negotiated the joys and sorrows, the ecstasies and existential angst, with a gentle assurance – and I want to acknowledge the wisdom and the positive encouragement of my community in this. Prayers on both sides go without saying, and these include the faithful, ordered liturgical remembrances and the personal commitment of sisters and brothers at a contemplative level.

As to the material aid, it is true that I earn money by writing and manual work, and I supply the monastery here with vegetables. But it has been affirmed that if a sister or brother were to pursue this path with no financial ability, it would make no difference. My huts, my food and basic needs are supplied, and, though they are modest, there is no question about availability.

Third, I owe my solitude to the community in that I live within the reciprocal circle of offering back to the monastic Church that which has been offered to me. My solitude is communal, for it is in God and within the communion of saints. There has been a pattern of light and darkness, and I have been confronted by dark powers in the intercessory and contemplative dimensions of prayer. But it is also true that I have been involved in the renewal of the image of God in my own life. I am experiencing, though still a beginner on the path, the transformation in Christ that the Orthodox Church calls theosis or divinization (2 Peter 1:4). There is an objective reality and a subjective appreciation in my experience of spirituality. The solitude in which this is possible is the gift which my community offers me, and which I accept with gratitude and return with joy.

In all this I am a microcosm. By that I mean that within myself is the whole monastic tradition, the whole Church and the whole world. I am here for God; I am here for the Church; I am here for the world. And I am here for myself – for, although I hope I am not pursuing an individualistic narcissism, I am certainly pursuing an intensely personal path – though in the fellowship of the communion of saints – on earth and in heaven.

And to get me grounded again, I must affirm an increasing sense of humour as to the ridiculousness of living alone in a series of wooden huts on a plot of ground in the middle of nowhere. And it is not simply being allowed, but positively encouraged. And for that I am immensely grateful!

Being firm and stubborn enough to affirm the vision of solitude on the one hand, and being pliable and humble enough to listen in trust and love to the community on the other: these are the two poles kept in creative tension by that opening paragraph of Merton's. So I shall conclude with another:

> 'The person who can live happily without snuggling up at every moment to some person, institution, or vice, is there as a promise of freedom to the rest of humankind. (Thomas Merton, *op. cit.* p 246)

The Hermitage, Glasshampton Monastery (drawn by Molly Dowell)

A Ministry of Welcome

by Sister Monica Popper SSM

In the summer of 1996, the Sisters of St Saviour's Priory, Haggerston, took the decision to give hospitality to refugees seeking asylum in the UK. Here, **Sister Monica** *looks at the difficulties current British regulations cause those fleeing from persecution in their own countries and shares her thoughts on all that the refugees have given to her Community.*

When, not so long ago, we described one facet of our Community's ministry as being a ministry of welcome, we little thought that this might include our providing a temporary home to two asylum seekers. As it is, this has been one of the most enriching experiences of the past few years.

St Margaret of Antioch, Haggerston Priory

As a result of regulations introduced by the previous Conservative government, and not so far repudiated by the present Labour administration, people seeking refuge in this country from persecution, torture and possible death, must register as refugees immediately on arrival in the UK if they are to receive state benefits which will enable them to survive while their case is being examined by the Home Office. Those who do not do this – whether out of fear of officialdom, ignorance of British procedures, inability to understand the language or any other reason – may, quite legally, remain until their status is decided, but they receive no state benefits, such as Income Support or Housing Benefit. Nor are they allowed to work for the first six months after applying for asylum. More often than not they are left destitute, without any means of supporting themselves. (This was the situation in the summer of 1996. Since then, the National Assistance Act of 1948 has been invoked, which obliges local authorities to house and give basic support to the destitute, and to some, not all, asylum seekers.)

As it was, in August 1996, the Refugee council was almost overwhelmed by asylum seekers without a roof, without food, clothing or money. The Community agreed that, on a short term basis, we could offer two rooms in our small Guest House – so long as these were not needed by anyone else: we could take two, for a maximum of four or five days, preferably two women.

On 10 September, two young men arrived: one a Christian from Cameroon and the other a Muslim from Algeria. Both were French-speaking. Come the weekend, when the time to send them back to the Refugee Council – and probably onto the streets – compassion had taken over. We had got to know them, tried out our halting French, joked a little and, above all, heard parts of their story. Surely they might stay on? Why should they not have precedence over other guests who might want to stay?

Remy, from Cameroon, went on to the Salvation Army and was replaced by Abdul from Afghanistan, aged just twenty, also a Muslim and with only limited command of English. Since then, our two 'boys' have been part of our extended family – the only family they now have.

Much learning and work have been needed on the practical level, especially at the beginning. Keeping up to date with asylum legislation, visits to the Immigration Office in Croydon (how is one supposed to get there without money?), registering with a doctor, applying for free medicines, finding suitable English classes . . . Mundane requirements such as clothing and suitable food had to be seen to, letters written to Members of Parliament and campaigning against inhuman regulations undertaken.

On top of this – where to get money? We were able to tap various charities as well as emptying the pockets of kind friends. Our aim has been to give the two young men a sense of independence and self-respect, insofar as that is possible – and it is difficult if you have no money in your pocket. Initially, this meant a small weekly sum from Community funds. However, as regulations changed, it has been possible to get more regular support from the local authority, after negotiating a nightmare of bureaucratic tangles, with no certainty that any arrangement will stay in place for more than a few weeks.

Even more demanding, and really only possible in the context of a supportive Community, is the need for human support and friendship. Imagine, like Athmane, you have left behind your parents and four brothers in Algiers. You can neither write nor phone them. An acquaintance, who has recently visited the country, tells you that your family has left the capital (you are relieved), and that your mother sends an urgent message: Under no circumstances are you to return as your life is in danger. Then you hear no more, but you listen to the radio and hear of almost daily massacres in Algeria. Or the other scenario, that of Abdul: your father has been shot dead because of your political involvement and your mother has handed over all the family money so that an agent can smuggle you out of Afghanistan into Pakistan and thence to Europe. The agent drops you at Heathrow and disappears. That is the last you know of your mother and your young brother, but the radio tells you of people fleeing Kabul, your home town, and of the barbarities of the Taleban.

That is the past. What of the future? When will your case be heard? Will you be given refugee status and allowed to remain or will you be deported? And the longer term – perhaps the most difficult thing of all for two gifted young men – what of a promising career, begun and now interrupted? What of the dreams of setting up a home, with a wife and family? Is this all now lost? No wonder that the incidence of suicide among asylum seekers is high and that befriending them is sometimes a heavy business.

There have been the good times also. Most memorable of these was the feast they prepared for the Sisters the first time they received money from the local council: a feast of thanksgiving. It needed two days of cooking and many shopping expeditions, but the resulting meal was magnificent. All their best foods from their homes were given to us – no expense spared. At the end of the meal, there was a presentation of gifts, splendidly wrapped: a big picture of the Last Supper and a statue of the Sacred Heart, both now kept on view in our Refectory.

There have been 'interfaith' events, quite spontaneously. Abdul danced for us at

Jesus poured water into a basin and began to wash the disciples' feet ... 'Do you know what I have done?', he said. 'If I, your Lord and Teacher, have washed your feet, you also ought to wash one another's feet.'
John 13. 5 & 14

Christmas – a graceful, impressive Afghani dance. For our part, we not only put on a party for his twenty-first birthday, but also celebrated the festival of Id-ul-Fitr, which marks the end of Ramadan, with a special meal.

How it will end, no one knows. It is to be hoped that the present inhumane asylum legislation will be abolished and be succeeded by more than just laws – and many continue to work for this. What we do know, in our Community, is that the presence of Athmane and Abdul in our house has been a gift. Our horizons have been widened, our imaginations kindled and a fresh understanding has been given to the words in the Gospel: 'When I was a stranger, you welcomed me.' It has turned out that the stranger, in whom we are to recognize the Lord, is not only a fellow human being, a brother or sister, but also a very valuable and lovable friend.

Indices

134

Index of Communities
by Dedication or Patron Saint

Index of Communities by Location
United Kingdom

Taplow (SPB)   74
Tymawr (SSC)   76
Walsall (CSP)   32
Walsingham (SSM)   92
Wantage (CSMV)   46
Warminster (CSD)   36
West Harrow (CSC)   55
West Malling (CHF)   27

West Malling (OSB)   69
Wetherby (OHP)   62
Whitby (OHP)   61
Windsor   *see Clewer*
Woking (CSP)   49
York (CSPH)   50
York (OHP)   62

Outside the UK

Australia
  Adelaide SA (SSM)   79
  Albion QLD (SSA)   102
  Brisbane QLD (SSF)   83
  Camperdown VIC (OSB)   98
  Cheltenham VIC (CHN)   102
  Diggers Rest VIC (SSM)   79
  Dondingalong NSW (CSC)   55
  East Burwood VIC (CSC)   55
  Glebe NSW (CSC)   55
  St Kilda VIC (CSC)   55
  South Oakleigh VIC (CHN)   102
  Stroud NSW (CC)   102
  Stroud NSW (SSF)   83
  Tabulam NSW (LBF)   102
  Wangaratta VIC (CCK)   102
  Wynn Vale SA (SI)   102
Bangladesh
  Barisal (BE)   101
  Barisal (CSS)   96
Canada
  Digby, Nova Scotia (SOLM)   56
  Edmonton, Alberta (SSJD)   105
  Hamilton, Ontario (CSC)   55
  Oakville, Ontario (CSC)   55
  Toronto, Ontario (OHC)   104
  Willowdale, Ontario (SSJD)   105
Dominican Republic
  San Petros de Macoris (CT)   104
Eire
  Dublin (CSJE)   102
France
  Var (CGA)   102
Fiji
  Suva (CSN)   102

Ghana
  Accra (OHP)   62
  Cape Coast (OHC)   101
Haiti
  Port-au-Prince (SSM)   106
India
  Calcutta (BE)   101
  Delhi (BAC)   101
  Kadampanad (CLG)   56
  Pune (CSMV)   48
Japan
  Tokyo (CN)   101
Korea
  Inchon (KFB)   101
  Pusan (OSB)   99
  Seoul (SHC)   99
Lesotho
  Leribe (CHN)   100
  Maseru (CHN)   100
  Maseru (SSM)   79
  Maseru (SPB)   101
Malaysia
  Sandakan, Sabah (CGS)   96
New Zealand
  Auckland (CSF)   39
  Auckland (SSF)   83
  Christchurch (CSN)   102
  Opononi (SLG)   57
  Wellington (CSN)   102
Papua New Guinea
  Goroka (CSVL)   97
  Goroka (SSF)   84
  Haruro (SSF)   84
  Hetune (CSVL)   97
  Lae (SSF)   84

Index of Communities by Initials

140

CSP	Community of St Peter, Woking	49
CSPH	Community of St Peter, Horbury	50
CSS	Christa Sevika Sangha	96
CSVL	Congregation of the Sisters of the Visitation of Our Lady	97
CSWG	Community of the Servants of the Will of God	52
CT	Community of the Transfiguration	103
CZR	Chita Che Zita Rinoyera	100
KFB	Korean Franciscan Brotherhood	101
LBF	Little Brothers of St Francis	102
MBH	Melanesian Brotherhood	102
MSH	Melanesian Sisterhood	102
OGS	Oratory of the Good Shepherd	59
OHC	Order of the Holy Cross, 101 & 104	
OHP	Order of the Holy Paraclete	61
OJN	Order of Julian of Norwich	104
OSA	Order of St Anne	104
OSB	Benedictine Community of St Benedict's Abbey, Bartonville	98
OSB	Benedictine Community of St Mark's Priory	98
OSB	Benedictine Community of Elmore Abbey	68
OSB	Benedictine Community of Our Lady and St John, Alton	64
OSB	Benedictine Community of St Mary's Abbey, West Malling	69
OSB	Benedictine Community at Pusan	99
OSB	Benedictine Community at Servants of Christ Priory, Phoenix	104
OSB	Benedictine Community of the Salutation of St Mary the Virgin, Burford	65
OSB	Community of St Mary at the Cross, Edgware	66
OSC	Community of St Clare	35
OSH	Order of St Helena	105
SC	Sisters of Charity	71
SE	Sisters of the Epiphany	72
SHC	Society of the Holy Cross	99
SHN	Sisterhood of the Holy Nativity	105
SHT	Society of the Holy Trinity	28
SI	Sisters of the Incarnation	102
SLG	Community of the Sisters of the Love of God	57
SOLM	Society of our Lady St Mary	56
SPB	Society of the Precious Blood, Lesotho	101
SPB	Society of the Precious Blood, UK	74
SSA	Society of the Sacred Advent	102
SSB	Society of the Sisters of Bethany	93
SSC	Society of the Sacred Cross	76
SSF	Society of St Francis	80
SSJD	Sisterhood of St John the Divine	105
SSJD	Society of St John the Divine	101
SSJE	Society of St John the Evangelist, UK	85
SSJE	Society of St John the Evangelist, USA	106
SSM	Society of the Sacred Mission	78
SSM	Society of St Margaret, Aberdeen	87

Index of Community Wares & Services for Sale

Look up the item or service you require and then contact the communities listed for more information. Their addresses can be found in the Directory section.

ALTAR BREAD
Benedictine Community of Our Lady and St John (Alton)   64
Community of St Clare (OSC)   35

BOOKS, PAMPHLETS & LEAFLETS
Community of the Holy Cross   25
Community of the Resurrection *(Leaflets on prayer)*   30
Community of St Clare (OSC)   35
Community of St John the Baptist   40
Community of the Servants of the Will of God   52
Community of the Sisters of the Love of God   57
Elmore Abbey   68
Society of St Francis   80

CALLIGRAPHY
Community of the Companions of Jesus the Good Shepherd   23

CANDLES
Community of the Companions of Jesus the Good Shepherd   23
Community of the Holy Name   28

CARDS
Benedictine Community of the Salutation (Burford)   65
Community of the Holy Cross   25
Community of the Holy Name   28
Community of St Clare (OSC)   35
Community of St Denys   36
Community of St John the Divine   42
Community of St Mary the Virgin   46
Community of St Peter   49
Community of the Sisters of the Church   54
Society of the Precious Blood   74
Society of St Francis   80
Society of St Margaret, Walsingham   92
Society of the Sisters of Bethany   93

CRAFTS
Community of the Holy Name (CHN)   28
Community of St Clare (OSC)   35
Community of St Laurence   44
Community of the Servants of the Will of God *(Jesus prayer ropes)*   52
Community of the Sisters of the Church   54
Society of the Precious Blood   74
Society of St Francis *(including prayer stools)*   80
Society of St Margaret, Walsingham   92

EMBROIDERY & CHURCH NEEDLEWORK
Community of the Companions of Jesus the Good Shepherd   23
Society of All Saints Sisters of the Poor   73

ICON PRINTS
Benedictine Community of the Salutation (Burford)   65
Community of the Servants of the Will of God   52

INCENSE
Elmore Abbey   68

PRINTING
Benedictine Community of the Salutation (Burford)   65
Community of St Clare (OSC)   35

Loyola Hall
Jesuit Spirituality Centre

Loyola Hall is well appointed with a prayerful chapel, six prayer rooms, group meeting rooms, art room, lounges, sauna, jacuzzi and large, beautiful grounds; easy access by road or public transport.

RETREATS AND COURSES
In 1998 we offer events on:

12 Step Spirituality	Psychosynthesis	Enneagram
Women's Spirituality	Healing	Men's Spirituality
Dream Retreat	Discernment	Lesbian & Gay	Story
Deaf Retirement	Singles	Clay & Art	Young Adults
Bereavement	Mid-Life Changes	Divorced or Separated
Beginners	Clergy	Religious Sisters and Brothers

Growth into Wholeness - a clergy retreat led by
Revd Andrew Walker and Fr David Birchall.   July 12-17, 1998

Enneagram Retreat - led by Fr. John McCluskey   July 17-24, 1998

Psychosynthesis Workshop & Retreat, led by Revd Andrew Walker
and Sr Kathleen Lyons   July 31-August 7, 1998

INDIVIDUALLY GUIDED RETREATS
These retreats are offered all the year round and can be taken over any period from 3 to 30 days.   *Please contact us for dates and availability.*

COURSES IN SPIRITUAL DIRECTION & PRAYER-GUIDANCE
Basic Prayer Guides Course -	Feb. 8-17, 1999
Seminar for Spiritual Guides & Retreat Givers -	Feb. 19-22, 1999
Basic Theology for Prayer Guides -	Feb. 24-28, 1999
Spiritual Accompaniment (Direction) -	March 8-21, 1999

For our programme, details of events, or to bring your own group:

**The Secretary,   Loyola Hall,   Warrington Rd,
Rainhill,   Prescot,   Merseyside,   L35 6NZ**
Tel: 0151 426 4137   Fax: 0151 431 0115
Email: loyola@clara.net   Web: http://home.clara.net/loyola

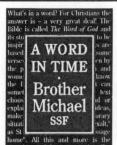 

WYDALE

'A PLACE FOR ALL REASONS IN ALL SEASONS'

Wydale Hall is situated 9 miles from Scarborough and near to the North Yorkshire moors. It is a gracious country house ideal for conferences, training courses, business seminars, holidays, retreats, quiet days, and 'time out'. Christmas and Easter House Parties and Walking Holidays.

Groups and individual guests are welcome!

There are 34 bedrooms, with accommodation for up to 68 guests, including a Chapel, a Conference Room, a Library Hall, a Lounge, a Sitting Room, a Dining Room, and a small Bar.

The Emmaus Centre is a separate unit providing self-catering accommodation for up to 30 guests. Primarily for young people, it is low-cost, centrally heated, and open all year round. Its **East Wing** provides accommodation for up to 16 physically handicapped guests plus 8 carers/leaders.

An all-weather floodlit multi-sports pitch is also available.

For further information please contact: Peter Fletcher, The Warden, Wydale, York Diocesan Centre, Brompton by Sawdon, Scarborough, North Yorkshire YO13 9DG. Tel: 01723 859270. Fax: 01723 859702. Registered Charity No. 244976